GOD, THE BIG BANG AND STE

'Dr Wilkinson has provided an exciting read in which he brings us to the frontiers of scientific thinking about the origin of the universe. He goes on to ask the question of how God relates to this scientific picture and through his own faith challenges us to get to know the God behind the universe in a personal way.'

Sir John Houghton, CBE, FRS

'David Wilkinson understands the work of Stephen Hawking and others on the origin of the universe, "from the inside". His description will help readers to understand the implications of the latest scientific research. His theological responses offer a way forward in what is less and less a battle, and more and more a conversation between science and theology. I commend this book most warmly as a contribution to the serious task of apologetics facing the Christian church today.'

Rev Dr Donald English

By the same author

In the Beginning God
Thinking Clearly About God and Science (with Rob Frost)

DAVID WILKINSON

GOD, THE BIG BANG and STEPHEN HAWKING

STRUIK CHRISTIAN BOOKS

MONARCH
Crowborough

First published 1993
Reprinted 1993
This edition 1996

British Library Cataloguing Data
A catalogue record for this book is available
from the British Library.

ISBN 1 85424 342 X

Co-published in South Africa with:
Struik Christian Books Ltd.,
Cornelis Struik House, 80 McKenzie Street,
Cape Town 8001, South Africa.
Reg no 04/02203/06

Designed and produced by Bookprint Creative Services
P.O. Box 827, BN21 3YJ, England for
MONARCH PUBLICATIONS
Broadway House, The Broadway
Crowborough, East Sussex, TN6 1HQ.
Printed in Great Britain.

To Alison
With my love

CONTENTS

FOREWORD

by Sir Arnold Wolfendale, FRS,
former Astronomer Royal

In his introduction to Stephen Hawking's book *A Brief History of Time*, Carl Sagan writes, 'This is a book about God . . . or perhaps about the absence of God.' What a contrast this makes with David Wilkinson's book, which is about the need for God, indeed the presence of God.

If anyone is fitted to write about the inter-relation of cosmology and religion it is Dr Wilkinson—a brilliant first degree in physics, followed by important research and a fine PhD in cosmology, and a degree in theology, comprise credentials of a high order. Clearly, the views of a writer with knowledge and experience in all these areas should command respect.

Of course, some will say that the arguments advanced in the book are too thin, but this is to miss the main point of the publication, which is to give a readable, yet informed overview and to stimulate discussion. My own view is that David Wilkinson *has* succeeded in this initial task and I hope that this success—surely to be manifested by a wide readership—will encourage readers to dig deeper into the great problems of God and the universe.

PREFACE

Does the universe have a beginning? And if it had a beginning, then what was its cause? Did God start it all off, and if he did can we know? These are the type of questions that fascinate both schoolchildren and university lecturers. Many people are intrigued by questions of origins, and in particular the origin of the universe.

This is a book which has arisen out of a lecture theatre rather than a study. For the past couple of years I have had the privilege of giving a lecture on cosmology and creation in a number of universities and colleges. The motivation for this lecture was to make accessible the ideas of modern physics on the origin of the universe, and to suggest that far from doing away with God, there was a new openness to religious questions within the scientific community.

The lecture was published by the Methodist Church Home Mission Division under the title '*In the beginning God?*'. This book is an expanded and revised version of that lecture, taking into account primarily the questions people raised. It is an attempt to present clearly to a reader with little background in science or religion the issues of the origin of the universe and God. I write as someone who has an unashamed enthusiasm both for science and the Christian faith. To some the approach will have too much science and not enough

Christianity. To others it will have too much Christianity and not enough science! To the first group, I would suggest that you really need to understand the science thoroughly if you are going to pose the right theological questions. To the second group, I would suggest that you need to be open to questions about God as they are inevitably raised by the science itself.

I owe a great deal of thanks to the many individuals throughout the country who have questioned and stimulated me into thinking a little more about these things. My work in theoretical astrophysics owes much to the inspiration of the Astronomer Royal, Professor A.W. Wolfendale, FRS. He advised me to do a PhD in astrophysics because the religious questions were clear to see. In that he was correct and I am grateful. Professor G.D. Rochester, FRS and my former collaborator Dr. N.C. Rana encouraged and supported me with patience and wisdom. My work on the relationship of science and Christianity has been greatly helped by support from and discussions with Rev. Dr. John Polkinghorne, FRS, Sir John Houghton, FRS, Sir Robert Boyd, FRS, Rev. Dr. Donald English, Dr. Oliver Barclay, Dr. Michael Poole, Professor Alan Millard, Rev. Ian Hill, Colin Goodman, Adam and Margaret Wilkinson, Deborah and Richard Horner, Rev. Brian Hoare and the numerous people who have questioned me at seminars and lectures.

This book would not have been possible without the help of Drs Rob and Liz Gayton and the support of the Methodist Church, in particular the congregation of Elm Hall Drive and the students of Liverpool University Methodist Society who have given me the time for lecturing and writing. Tony and Jane Collins encouraged me to write the book and have been supportive and skilful publishers.

Dr. Andrew Fox drew the excellent cartoons, while Alison Wilkinson, Dr. Mark Kermode, Rev. Dr. Ian Carter, and Alan Cresswell provided useful comments on the manuscript, although errors that remain are the sole responsibility of the author!

Finally, my wife Alison has endured the writing of a book during the first year of our married life! She has done so with graciousness, humour and sacrificial support. Her theological wisdom and practical help have been invaluable. She has loved me and shown me more of Jesus.

David A. Wilkinson, Liverpool, February 1993.

PREFACE TO NEW EDITION

It is a pleasure to acknowledge the help of Alison Wilkinson, Dr Mark Kermode, Jamie Probin and James Twynham in the writing of the extra chapter and compiling the index.

David A. Wilkinson
December 1995

CHAPTER ONE

WHY SUCH A BIG INTEREST?

The Big Bang is a big business. Although this theory of the origin of the universe has been around for some time it is only in recent years that it has become the source of intense scientific research, theological speculation and great public interest. As science has probed deeper and further into the history of the universe, so it has raised questions which reach far beyond its own domain.

Much of the popular interest can be attributed directly to one book, which has been a publishing phenomenon of our time. Stephen Hawking's *A Brief History of Time*[1] in which he explores the cosmological theories of the universe has enjoyed unusual success. Most books on cosmology are confined to a rather select clientele who visit the astronomy section of reputable book stores. In spite of the publisher's initial expectations, Hawking's work has never been so confined.

When launched in 1988 it captured the public imagination in a way that would keep it on the best-seller list for well over three years. As a hardback it has sold over 600,000 copies in Britain and 5.5 million copies worldwide. It has inspired newspaper articles, theological papers, a Readers' Guide, a television film and even a film about the making of the television film! This last production is an honour normally reserved for such pinnacles of human creativity as *Star Wars* and *Raiders of the Lost Ark*!

This raises the inevitable question of why such a response? Why does this book rival *The Country Diary of an Edwardian Lady* for the nation's most popular hardback? Why should a book which deals with such 'everyday' concepts as 26 dimensional spaces and quantum theories of gravity become one of the standard coffee table books of our generation? Why should a science hardback inspire so many people who gave up science after being bemused by third form physics to struggle their way through modern theories of cosmology?

The answers to these questions are not easy. As C.P. Snow remarked some years ago, in the nation's 'two cultures' an ignorance about science is far more acceptable than an ignorance about literature. In addition, Hawking writes about some extremely difficult concepts. When someone like Bernard Levin admits in his column in *The Times* that he was unable to get beyond page 29 of the book, one wonders whether *A Brief History* rivals the Bible for the book that everyone has but has never fully read!

Part of the answer is surely due to Stephen Hawking himself. He writes with an engaging clarity, introducing the wonders of science without recourse to mathematics. He communicates his own excitement with the subject. Perhaps as important, is the fact that he writes out of a personal story which has gripped the public's sympathy and admiration. His courageous struggle with motor neurone disease for nearly 30 years after being told he only had two and a half years to live, his rise to Lucasian Professor of Mathematics at Cambridge, his original scientific work and his popularizing of that science despite being confined to a wheelchair and voice synthesizer is one of those rare human stories. He has become a media personality, hailed as the greatest scientist since Albert Einstein, and his recent 50th birthday received a Hollywood-type fanfare.

However, that is not the whole story of the book's appeal. Recent biographies of Hawking have come nowhere near *A Brief History* in terms of sales. To say that the public interest is just in Hawking, does him the disservice of not taking seriously the questions that he is engaging. I believe that there are two important reasons which lie outside Hawking's personal story. It is these two reasons which have a more lasting significance and a central place in the history of human thought. They are the question of origins and the question of God.

The question of origins

Hawking's work is about origins. The aim of his cosmological theory is for a complete description of the universe by means of a single theory, a theory that not only explains how the universe changes with time but also what the initial conditions were.

From the very beginning of time it seems, humanity has asked such questions as 'Why are we here?' and 'What is our significance?' The answer to such questions has often led to the question of origins, as if in the attempt to explain where we come from we may find the clue to locating ourselves in the universe.

Of course, this has not only been the domain of science. The religions of the world make their own claims as to the nature of the universe and its origins. The Babylonian epic 'Enuma Elish' dating from before 1100BC speaks of the origin of the universe as part of a cosmic battle between the gods. Men and women are created from the blood of the god Kingu with the specific purpose of serving the host of gods. This story seemed to be primarily a literary monument to the god Marduk, showing how he was supreme among all gods. However, this does not take away the fact that the Babylonians were dealing with questions of origins. It was not enough to give an account of the world by saying that each part was ruled by different gods. The account needed an origin.

As we shall see, although the Judaeo-Christian account of the nature of the world is very different to the Babylonian account, it too takes seriously the question of origins. Represented primarily in the early chapters of the book of Genesis it sees the significance of human beings in terms of their intimate relationship with the one God who had brought them and the whole universe into being.

Certainly in our own day accounts of origins have great fascination and importance within society. Richard Dawkins, Reader in Zoology at the University of Oxford, attracted widespread interest when in giving the 1991 BBC Royal Institution Christmas Lectures he made a passionate defence of evolutionary biology. Charles Darwin's *The Origin of Species* stands as one of the most famous books of human history. It gave birth to the theory of evolution in the biological sphere, showing that natural selection through the influence of the environment could explain the adaptation of living organisms. Such a view is not without controversy even today, but became the focus of the battle between religion and science in the nineteenth century, particularly when humanity was seen to be descended from apes. The power and controversy of evolution, it may be argued, come from its attempt to explain our origin.

Today the story goes much further than apes. Watson and Crick have elucidated the structure of DNA showing how genetic inheritance is passed through generations. In the 1950s experiments at the University of Chicago with gases and electric sparks suggested the possibility of the emergence of amino-acids from the 'primeval soup' of the early terrestrial atmosphere.

However, for all the interest in biological evolution there is a yet more fundamental question. This question is perceived to be of such importance that society gives millions of pounds and thousands of scientists to it. It is the question of the origin of the universe. If we come from amino-acids, then where do the atoms come from which make such complex molecules? And when I gaze at the sky what is the origin of all the billions of stars that I see?

It is a great question. On the 24th April 1992 newspapers, television and radio went wild about ripples. From tabloid headlines to intellectual chat shows 'the secret of the universe' was said to have been found. The whole story revolved around data collected by a satellite called COBE (the cosmic background explorer). The ripples that COBE had found were taken as evidence of the seeds from which galaxies had formed after the Big Bang. Project scientist George Smoot claimed 'it is going to change our view of the universe and our place within it'. He received international stardom overnight and an offer of up to $2 million to write a book about the discovery.

The importance of this discovery was that it seemed to be the last piece of the jigsaw needed for the whole picture of the Big Bang. This is the theory of the origin of the universe which says that the universe expanded from a size small enough to fit through the eye of a needle to its present size over some 15 billion years. The COBE ripples however were a cause for a sigh of relief rather than great rejoicing for the majority of cosmologists. If they had not been found then certain theories of galaxy formation would have had to have been revised.

What is significant is that this relatively moderate discovery was hailed as the answer to life, the universe and everything! Whether the story was hyped by those without enough news, or by those without enough research grants will remain an open question. The story was about origins and that grabbed attention.

Leo Tolstoy wrote in *War and Peace*,[2] 'The highest wisdom has but one science—the science of the whole—the science explaining the whole creation and man's place in it.' It is this explanation of the origin of everything which Hawking addresses and which finds such a resonance with the public imagination.

A question about God

There was a time when to write about science and God in the same book was reserved only for theologians or eccentrics trying to argue that Jesus was a spaceman. Today it seems all the rage, and the Big Bang has played no small part in this.

In 1951, Pope Pius XII, on the basis of work on the Big Bang by Catholic cosmologists such as Milne and Whitaker, suggested that such a model was in full agreement with Catholic dogma:

> Thus with that concreteness which is characteristic of physical proofs, it [science] has confirmed the contingency of the universe and also the well founded deduction as to the epoch [some five billion years ago] when the cosmos came forth from the hands of the Creator. Hence, creation took place in time. Therefore, there is a Creator.[3]

Now we might expect such an attitude from those who are fully convinced Christians. What has been surprising has been the importance of the God question for those scientists without any formal Christian allegiance.

Professor Paul Davies, a theoretical physicist at Adelaide University, has pursued the relationship of God and the origin of the universe in a series of books and articles. In 1983 in his book *God and the New Physics*[4] he even argued that science offers a surer path to God than religion. Sir Fred Hoyle, a long time critic of Christian faith, also in 1983 wrote a book entitled *The Intelligent Universe*[5] in which he pursued the line of an intelligent design behind the universe. These books are a sign of an increasing dialogue between science and religion.

Some have even gone as far as to speak of a revival of natural theology, that is, the attempt to know God through inspection and reflecting upon the universe.

Now in this God does not always do too well. The atheist Richard Dawkins recently attacked Archbishop John Habgood at the Edinburgh Science Festival on the subject of religion. However, the subsequent correspondence in the newspapers bore testimony to how alive this subject is. The television series *Soul* presented by Anthony Clare highlighted a whole number of points of contact between science and religion. More and more people in Western society demonstrate that there is more to life than just what science tells us, whether it be by astrology, New Age, science fiction or indeed religion.

The 'God question' is certainly an important part of Hawking's work. Carl Sagan, the astrophysicist and popularizer of science, characterizes *A Brief History of Time* in his foreword as,

> a book about God . . . or perhaps about the absence of God . . . The word God fills these pages . . . a universe with no edge in space, no beginning or end in time, and nothing for a Creator to do.[6]

Popular reviews of Hawking have often presented him as disproving God or at least saying that in his system of thought there is no room for God. Later in this book we shall make clear that the place of God in Hawking's picture is a little more subtle than such views. It is perhaps enough at present simply to note that the question of origins raises the God question.

Does the Big Bang have to start in any particular way? What came before the Big Bang? Does the universe need a beginning at all? Is God needed to start the whole thing off by lighting the blue touch paper of the Big Bang?

These questions need to be addressed. They are about a quest for origins and about a quest for God. In this we need to take seriously what science tells us about the structure, evolution and origin of the universe. We also need to take God seriously. If a recurring phenomenon of intellectual history is to link understanding of humanity, the divine and the world, we shall look for such a link in the origin of the universe.

In chapters 2 to 6 we will try to clearly state the development of scientific thinking concerning the origin of the universe. This will involve us in thinking not just about the results of science but also its method. Then in the second part of the book, we will examine what the Christian view of God both gives and receives in relation to the scientific view.

Who lit the blue touch paper? Was it God, or did it light itself?

CHAPTER TWO

SPACE ... THE FINAL FRONTIER?

'That's one small step for man, a giant leap for mankind', declared Neil Armstrong as he stepped from the ladder of Apollo 11 onto the surface of the Moon. In fact, by missing out the 'a' before 'man' he rendered the sentence meaningless, but the sentiment certainly summarized the achievement. This achievement of enabling Armstrong and Aldrin to land on the surface of the Moon and return safely to the Earth, was not just a testimony to technology, it symbolized humanity's quest to reach out into a vast universe.

This $25 billion Apollo program has had profound effects. It inspired a whole generation in science and technology. In one sense everything from non-stick frying pans to *Star Trek* came out of the program. It also highlighted the question of God. Yuri Gegarin returned from space to proclaim that he had not found God, but millions watched television as the Apollo astronauts circled the Moon reading the first chapter of the Bible, 'In the beginning, God created the heavens and the earth.'

The question is, by stepping out into the universe has humanity left God behind or is he there to be seen in a new way? Of course, the Apollo program was only one small part of humanity's quest to reach out into the universe. The universe has been a source of fascination which has provoked art, religion and science. For example, Halley's comet was observed by the Babylonians in 164BC, was noted as an omen in the Bayeaux Tapestry, was painted by Giotto over the stable of Christ's birth, was used by Halley to demonstrate Newton's law of gravitation, has been examined by telescopes and satellites and has even been the subject of songs and novels! And that is just one comet.

Let us begin by reviewing what kind of universe we have encountered in modern science.

A small step of 240,000 miles

If many are tempted to say in this age of technology and communication that it is a small world, then the universe gives a different perspective. Armstrong's step onto the Moon was 240,000 miles away from Cape Kennedy. Now that is not too far, being the equivalent of doing the journey between London and Liverpool some thousand times. As Fred Hoyle has remarked, space is only half an hour's drive away if your car could go straight up!

However, such a journey is a very small step in astronomical terms: 'Space is big. Really big. You just won't believe how vastly mindbogglingly big it is. I mean you may think it is a long way down the road to the chemist, but that's just peanuts to space.'

So began that 'classic' of modern astronomy *The Hitchhiker's Guide to the Galaxy*[7]. On this point it was quite correct. Do the journey to the Moon and back some 200 times, and you get the distance to the Sun, just under 100 million miles. The Sun is orbited by nine planets with over sixty moons, with a great number of asteroids and comets. To give some sense of scale, if you imagine the Sun to be the size of a peanut located in London, then the Earth would be a speck of dust about half a metre away, the outermost planet Pluto would be 20 metres away, and the nearest star would be another peanut in Sheffield. Space is an extremely empty frontier.

In order to talk of what is beyond the solar system without having this book full of pages of zeros after each number, astronomers speak of distances in terms of light years. This is the distance travelled by light, at its constant speed of approximately 300,000,000 metres per second, over the time of one year. Using these units the distance to the nearest star, Proxima Centauri is about four light years.

Proxima Centauri and our Sun are amongst the stars that make up the Milky Way Galaxy. This group of stars is visible on a clear night, if you can get away from street lighting, as a diffuse band of light across the sky. It contains 100 billion stars grouped together in a spiral pattern in a thin disc.

We are located about two thirds of the distance away from the centre of the disc. The total diameter of the Milky Way is 100,000 light years. By multiplying this number by the 9.5 trillion kilometres (which is the distance of one light year) you can work out after the half hour it takes for your car to get into space, how long it would take to do a round trip!

As you might expect the story does not end there. The nearest galaxy to us can be seen from the southern hemisphere. It is called the Large Magellanic Cloud and is at a distance of 160,000 light years. At one tenth the size of the Milky Way, it is quite a small galaxy, having a mere 10 billion stars!

Galaxies come in all shapes and sizes. The Large Magellanic Cloud has no discernible pattern and is classed as an irregular galaxy. Some like M87 are huge elliptical galaxies while others such as Leo I are called dwarf spheroidals for obvious reasons. Some seem to be bright and young, others have very active sources of radiation at their centres, and some are in the process of being ripped apart by their neighbours. Galaxies themselves group together in vast clusters like the Virgo cluster over distances of millions of light years. The movement of

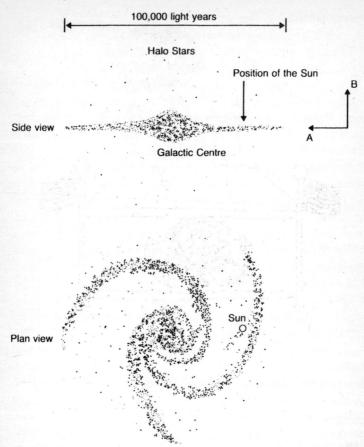

Fig 2.1 Diagram of the Milky Way Galaxy. From the side it appears as a thin disc with a central concentration of stars called the Galactic Centre. The position of the Sun is about two thirds of the radius from the centre. If you imagine that you are in the disc, then the directions of observation A and B illustrate why the Milky Way as viewed from Earth appears to be a band of stars across the sky. Observing along A you will see lots of stars as a band, while observing in direction B you see fewer stars. The plan view of the Galaxy shows the stars grouped into a spiral pattern.

Fig 2.2 An American Dream?

galaxies around one another in such clusters is well described by the force of gravity.

Recently, claims have been made of sightings of clusters of galaxies and very bright galaxies called quasars at distances of billions of light years. The measurement of distances in astronomy has been and still is a difficult problem. One or two astronomers have contested such claims, but all are agreed that the universe stretches for billions of light years.

Assuming that the galaxies we observe are a representative sample of the distribution of galaxies in the universe, we can calculate the total number of galaxies. The numbers are so vast, that there are more stars than grains of sand on the beaches of the world.

It is said that a former President of the United States used to go through a ritual to stop himself becoming too proud.

Before going to bed he would go outside the White House and locate the constellation of Pegasus. He would say, 'One of those lights is the spiral galaxy of Andromeda. It contains one hundred billion stars each the size of our own Sun. It is one of one hundred billion galaxies in the universe, each as large as our own Milky Way Galaxy.' Then he would pause for a moment and say, 'Now I feel small enough, I can go to bed!'

The thing that is only half an hour away by car can be both frightening and fascinating. The vastness of the universe has been revealed by science in ways undreamed of by those who simply gazed at the sky. It certainly should make humanity humble.

Nevertheless, however big or however complex the universe is, the remarkable history of modern astronomy shows that it is comprehensible. We can reach out in understanding the vastness of the universe, but we can also reach deeper into the physics of what it is and how it evolves.

Twinkle, twinkle little star . . .

The task of NASA engineers was to propel Apollo 11 at a speed of 24,791 miles per hour from the Earth to the Moon. This was not a trivial matter. The Moon was orbiting the Earth, the command capsule had to orbit the Moon while the lander touched down, the two had to meet up again, and then the three astronauts had to be returned to Earth. It needed a lot of engineering and a great deal of computing, but was only possible because of the laws of physics. Among many other things, the Moon's orbit and gravitational field had to be determined, the fuel load calculated, and the launch time specified.

This is possible because of the ability of science to observe

Fig 2.3 *Nursery astronomy!*

and understand the universe. It makes possible the answer to the question, 'Twinkle, twinkle little star, how I wonder what you are.'

A star is a hot ball of hydrogen gas undergoing nuclear fusion. How do we know this? After all the twinkling of a star does not convey such a picture. A Celtic blessing says, 'Deep peace of the shining stars to you.' Unfortunately nothing could be further from the truth, for stars are very violent objects.

They may appear to be peaceful, but even the twinkling is an effect of the atmosphere of our Earth rather than intrinsic to stars themselves. Only as science has put together theory and observation, have stars been opened up to us.

The nearest star is of course our Sun. Its light enables the atmosphere of the Earth to sustain life. The light from the Sun which we see with our eyes is only a small part of the so-called electromagnetic spectrum. As white light passes through a water droplet in the atmosphere it splits up into its constituent colours from red to violet. This is how a rainbow forms. Each colour represents a different wavelength of electromagnetic radiation. We see the colours because our eyes are sensitive to those particular wavelengths. However, also in the spectrum of electromagnetic radiation are wavelengths or 'colours' beyond the red and beyond the violet. We cannot see them with our eyes but their effects are important and we can measure them with instruments. Beyond visible red light at longer wavelengths are infra-red radiation, microwaves and radio waves. At shorter wavelengths than violet are ultra-violet radiation, X-rays and gamma-rays.

Superimposed upon this series of wavelengths, are a number of dark lines, called spectral lines. The analysis of these spectral lines allows the determination of the temperature and chemical composition of the star.

From such an analysis, we know that the Sun is a hot ball of mainly hydrogen gas. However, where does its energy come from? In the mid nineteenth century, Herman von Helmholtz and Lord Kelvin suggested that a ball of gas contracting under the force of gravity would produce energy and this was the source. This is indeed true but calculations show that this would sustain the Sun for only 15 million years. Geological evidence indicates that the Sun has been radiating energy for much longer, a few billion years. This means that there must be another source of energy.

It was not until earlier this century that such a source was discovered. The source is nuclear fusion. This process, which gives the hydrogen bomb its destructive power, produces energy when the nuclei of light atoms such as hydrogen or helium fuse together into new elements. So in one sense the Sun is a carefully balanced H-bomb!

It was formed when a cloud of hydrogen began to collapse under the force of gravity. As the gravitational force makes parts of the cloud contract so the pressure in those parts increases. As the pressure increases so does the temperature (that is why a bicycle pump heats up when used). When the temperature reaches 10,000,000 K[8] then hydrogen nuclei fuse together to become helium, and this internal energy source supports the young star against further gravitational collapse.

By turning to different wavelengths of electromagnetic radiation with telescopes and satellites, it is possible to observe such a process happening today. The famous Orion nebula is one such region where stars are being born. It can just be seen as a misty patch around the central star of the three which form Orion's sword. Four young bright stars around a million years old (barely out of the midwife's arms in stellar terms) are pumping out their energy into the remaining gas of the original cloud producing a colourful and visually stunning region. Its brightness led to it being the first such nebula to be photographed in the 1880s.

If that is the beginning of a star's life then what about its end? A star uses up its available hydrogen fuel over a period of millions to billions of years depending on its size. This spells death for the star. As the hydrogen is used up, the core of the star contracts further. When a temperature of 100,000,000 K is reached the helium nuclei fuse to form carbon and oxygen. This process continues depending on the size of the star until elements up to iron are synthesized.

As this is occurring, the outer layers of the star begin to expand in order to balance the internal pressure and gravitational forces, and the star swells up in its desperate need to keep going. However, this 'red giant' phase cannot go on, and gravity eventually takes over.

For a star similar to the Sun, the outer layers of gas are shed (this is called a planetary nebula) while the inner core contracts to a small dense object called a white dwarf. A white dwarf is about the size of a planet but a million times heavier.

For a star more massive than the Sun, the contraction under gravity is more violent and the star explodes in what is termed a supernova. Such an explosion was observed on the 4th July 1054 leaving behind the remnants which Lord Rosse discovered in 1844, known as the Crab Nebula. Chinese astronomers saw it explode and it was so bright that it was visible in the day-time sky for three weeks. There is a lot of speculation on why the event was not recorded by European astronomers. Some think it was due to religious authorities suppressing the record, but a simpler (and not at all unlikely) explanation was that it was cloudy in Europe for that time! Such an explosion violently throws out gas into space at speeds greater than 1,000 kilometres per second and leaves behind a much smaller and denser object called a neutron star. Such neutron stars are approximately 20 miles across. They derive their name from the neutrons which are formed out of protons and electrons combined in the intense pressure.

On the 23rd February 1987, some of the debris from a supernova explosion arrived on the Earth. This supernova was the closest to the Earth for 383 years, but even then the actual explosion had taken place some 150,000 years ago. This supernova, named Supernova 1987A, was observed simultaneously from Chile and New Zealand, and its effects are still being studied. Its 'debris' consisted of particles called neutrinos which do not interact very much at all with the atoms in our bodies—in fact, they pass through us all the time without our being aware of them.

A combination of rotation and intense magnetic fields leads to some of these remnants being seen as pulsars. Jocelyn Bell and her PhD supervisor, Anthony Hewish, at Cambridge were the first to detect regular pulses of radiation from a particular point in the sky. These pulses were even considered to be an extra-terrestrial intelligence attempting contact, but were eventually shown to be a 'lighthouse effect' from pulsars. The magnetic fields focus a beam of radiation in a particular direction, and if the Earth is orientated so that this beam sweeps past it due to the rotation of the pulsar, the radiation will appear to be a series of pulses, rather like the regular beam of a lighthouse. It should be noted that pulsars rotate very quickly. The one at the centre of the Crab has a rotation rate of 30 times per second.

It is in the intense explosions of supernovas that the heavier elements such as gold and uranium are formed. This exploded material, now containing all the ninety-two elements of the periodic table, is mixed with more hydrogen and helium before the next generation of stars is formed. Thus our Sun, and the planets which formed with it, are made out of previous stellar material. The atoms of carbon which make up our bodies were once made in the nuclear furnace of a long-vanished star. In one sense, we are all made of the ashes of dead stars.

Before we leave the fate of stars however, we must mention one other possibility which will have great importance for the origin of the universe. For stars greater than about 50 times the mass of the Sun, the collapse is so violent that even neutron pressure cannot stop it and a black hole is formed. This object is so dense that the gravity it exerts is able to stop light escaping from its surface. Such a possibility had been suggested as long ago as the eighteenth century, but not until recently have scientists had the capability to try and detect a black hole.

The problem is, of course, that if the black hole's gravitational field is so intense that no radiation or matter can escape, then there is no way of detecting it directly. The search for black holes must therefore centre on their indirect effects. There are a number of possibilities. Many stars exist as binary stars, that is two stars orbiting around each other. If one star becomes a black hole it would have an effect on its neighbour. It may be that the motion of the remaining star as viewed from the Earth would appear unusual, as it would be orbiting around an unseen companion. Alternatively, the black hole through its gravitational force could be ripping material out of the atmosphere of its companion. However, matter does not fall directly into the black hole, but forms a rotating disc, spiralling into the hole. In such an accretion disc, the frictional forces are so strong that it is expected that X-rays are given off and these can be detected. Finally, the intense gravity of a black hole may bend the path of light from stars behind the black hole on its way to Earth. Such a bending can produce the appearance of a double image, and the search for 'doubles' could provide the evidence for black holes.

This is just part of the incredible universe that astronomy has opened up. From Galileo's use of the telescope in 1610 to observe the moons of Jupiter, to the recently launched space telescope, observation has played a key role. Information carried by all the different parts of the electromagnetic spectrum which comes to the Earth from the farthest corners of the universe has given us a picture of vastness, dynamic activity and complexity. And yet it is a picture that we can increasingly understand. The laws of physics have enabled us to understand stars, black holes and the structure of galaxies. However, can they enable us to understand the very origin of the universe itself?

CHAPTER THREE

FROM THE VERY BIG TO THE VERY SMALL

Where did it all come from? If the carbon which is in my body comes from supernova explosions, and supernova explosions come from stars, and stars come from clouds of hydrogen, then where does the hydrogen come from in the first place? Is it even possible for creatures who live on a planet which orbits a star in a rather insignificant place in a rather insignificant galaxy to understand how this vast and complex universe arose? The search for the answer to that question has a history stretching back to the ancient Greeks and beyond, and forms one of the most exciting stories of the development of human thinking. Modern science has been driven to the conclusion that the answer lies in an event which is commonly called the 'Big Bang'. This term was coined by one of the most vehement critics of the Big Bang, Sir Fred Hoyle, as a term of derision for a theory that he described as being about as elegant as a party girl jumping out of a cake! However, this inelegant theory has become the foundation of modern cosmology.

Science has made some astonishing discoveries, whether it be the role of DNA as the store of genetic information or the structure of atoms in terms of electrons and quarks. However these remarkable descriptions of modern science pale into

Fig 3.1 A long time ago!

insignificance compared to the astonishing picture that is presented when talking about the origin of the universe. Modern cosmologists, that is those who study the structure and evolution of the universe, believe that they can give a good description of the universe from the present day to an age when it was only a split second old.

In fact current scientific theories describe the universe back to a time when it was only 10^{-43} seconds old (which is a shorthand way of writing 1 divided by 10 followed by 42 zeros, that is: 1/1000000000000000000000000000000000000000000th of a second—which is a pretty small fraction!).

At that stage, some 15 billion years ago, everything in the universe, all the matter that will be in the billions of stars in billions of galaxies, was an incredibly dense mass. In fact it was so small that it could pass through the eye of a needle. The whole universe in diameter was of the order of 10^{-33}cm. From that point it expanded very rapidly. The expansion was

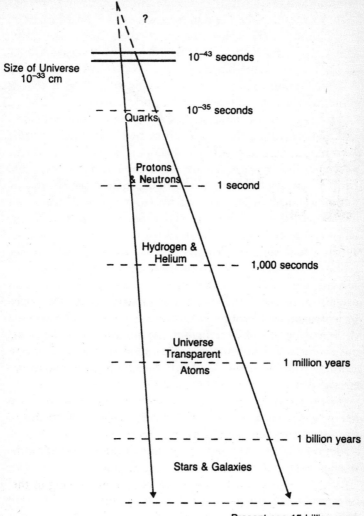

Fig 3.2 A Brief History of the Big Bang. The evolution of the universe, but not to scale! The solid lines show where our present laws of physics apply, and the broken lines where they break down.

so rapid and so violent that it is helpful to think of it in terms of an explosion—the Big Bang. However, we must be careful of the term, as an explosion suggests the sense of something that creates destruction and disorder. It also suggests 'bits' flying out into something, which we will see is not the case. A better picture may be the blooming of a flower, that is something that gives rise to order and beauty.

At this point the universe was at extremely high pressures and temperatures, the temperature being an unimaginable 10^{32} K. As the universe expanded, so it cooled, by the same principle that the expansion of carbon dioxide in a fire extinguisher cools. At 10^{-35} seconds, quarks which are the building blocks of protons and neutrons appeared. At about a hundredth of a second into the universe's life, the temperature was still so high (100 billion K) that not even atoms could survive. Protons and neutrons, which are the building blocks with electrons of atoms, appeared after one second. Only after three minutes did the temperature cool down enough (to less than a billion degrees!) for the nuclei of hydrogen and helium to form, to leave the universe with 76% hydrogen and 24% helium. Apart from small amounts of lithium and deuterium, that was all at that stage. The rest of the elements were to be formed much later in stars. The overall density was now about ten times the density of water.

It took a further million years for the universe to cool down so that electrons could be added to these nuclei to form atoms. In this formation of atoms an opaque universe became transparent. This is due to the fact that up to this point photons of light were continually interacting with matter. A similar effect gives the reason why it is impossible to see into the interior of the Sun, as light from the centre interacts with matter and does not come straight out.

As the universe cools further, so hydrogen clouds form stars and galaxies over billions of years. It is truly the story of the very big from the very small.

Pointers from the past

The question is, how can we know that all this is true? When God said to Job, 'Where were you when I laid the earth's foundation?' (Job 38:4), we are tempted to ask the same thing. Of course scientists only appeared on the scene 15 billion years after the Big Bang, never mind the first few seconds. This is an important point.

However, we can look back in time. This is because light travels at a finite speed. The television pictures from Apollo 11 took just over one second to reach the Earth from the Moon. Light from the Sun takes about eight and a half minutes to reach us. Therefore, when we look at the most distant galaxies, we see them as they were 10 billion years ago, as it has taken that length of time for their light to travel to us. This is useful but it can never get us back to the Big Bang as the astronomer hits the barrier when the universe was about one million years old and light was scattered. This acts as an opaque wall stopping us from receiving information from the Big Bang directly.

Thus cosmology is a little different to the rest of physics in that it deals with a unique event which happened in the past. You cannot ask a physics undergraduate to expand a universe in the laboratory and study it! Cosmology is more like a detective story, or historical investigation. It is about attempting to put together various clues or pieces of evidence in order to reconstruct what actually happened. The only trouble is that the 'crime' took place billions of years ago.

General relativity

At the end of the nineteenth century, many physicists believed that they would soon be out of a job. Physics had solved almost everything, or so they thought. Only two fundamental problems remained. The first was the detection of the so-called ether, and the second was the radiation from a heated body. These 'small' problems of the nineteenth century would in fact lead to the two major theories of twentieth century physics, general relativity and quantum theory. The Big Bang is built on general relativity, and quantum theory could provide the solution to one of its major problems.

The problem of the ether was to detect the medium through which light waves travelled. James Clerk Maxwell had united electricity and magnetism in an elegant theory showing that light could be understood as a wave motion of electric and magnetic fields. But waves need something to travel through. It was known that light travels through a vacuum, so there had to be something else which pervaded everywhere, the ether.

Michaelson and Morley attempted to show that the speed of light would be different in two directions due to the Earth's motion through this postulated ether, but they found that the speed of light did not vary at all. It was this surprising result that led a young patent office clerk to one of the great theories of modern physics. Albert Einstein saw that talk about the ether was unnecessary, but what was important was that the speed of light was the same however you measured it. This was the basis of his Special Theory of Relativity. He argued that for all observers not undergoing acceleration, the laws of physics should be the same. The result of this was the abandonment of absolute time. Einstein argued that one's measurement of time depended on one's motion. Clocks travelling at speeds close to the speed of light would appear to run slower than those at rest. Other bizarre consequences were that as speed increases, so mass increases and length contracts. These effects only become obvious at speeds close to the speed of light—at an everyday level they are so small that we do not notice them. In such a picture, time is not to be totally divorced from space, but the two are to be talked about together in a framework called 'space-time'.

Then in 1915, after ten years' work, Einstein published his General Theory of Relativity. His Special Theory had not taken gravity into account. In his General Theory not only was gravity included, but he also gave a brilliant new description of it. He suggested that space-time was not fixed and permanent, but could be described as being shaped by the presence in it of material bodies like stars and planets. Imagine a rubber sheet stretched flat. If a heavy object like a stone is placed upon it, the sheet changes shape. The flatness is replaced by a curved surface. A smaller object like a golf ball placed on the sheet will not be static but will roll towards the stone. It appears to be attracted by the stone, which of course is what gravity is all about. Einstein had given a geometric description of the law of gravity. The mass and distribution of matter in the universe determines the geometry of space and the rate of flow of time.

This complex interaction of matter and space-time was described by a set of equations, whose solution gave the geometry of space-time and showed how bodies moved within it. However, they were so difficult that they could only be solved in a few simple cases. One of these was for a uniform distribution of structureless points freely floating in space-time. Such a case is in fact a good approximation to the universe, since when taken as a whole, the clusters of galaxies have a relatively uniform distribution.

Almost immediately, the Dutch astronomer Willem de Sitter and the Russian mathematician Alexander Friedmann showed that the theory predicted that the universe was not static but expanding. Of course, if it was expanding then it must have expanded from something, it must have had a beginning. Einstein however was disturbed by such a conclusion and in a letter to de Sitter wrote, 'This circumstance [of an expanding universe] irritates me.' He was even tempted to modify the equations in order to make the universe static, but this he claimed later was the 'biggest blunder of my life'.

As these theorists pondered the equations, others were observing the universe, and coming to the same conclusion.

The redshift of galaxies

A galaxy, because of its constituent stars and gas, emits light in a characteristic spectrum. In 1912 at the Lowell Observatory in Flagstaff, Arizona, Vesto Melvin Slipher was investigating such spectra. He observed that for certain galaxies key features in the spectrum were all shifted towards the red part of the spectrum. This is what is called redshift. A similar effect occurs as we listen to a car pass under us while standing on a bridge over a motorway. The pitch of the sound of the car is higher when it is approaching compared to when it is moving away, and indeed depends on the speed. The redshifts of galaxies told Slipher that they were all moving away from us at speeds greater than 1,000 kilometres per second.

He reported his findings at a meeting of the American Astronomical Society in 1914, a year before Einstein's Theory of Relativity. At the end of his paper an astonishing thing happened. Everyone stood and cheered, which is not quite in character with the coldness of scientific meetings! At this point its full significance was not clear, but it was obvious that there was something very special in his work.

However, to interpret this information the distances to these galaxies were needed. This is not as simple as it sounds and indeed is one of the longstanding problems of astronomy. For distances about 10 times further than 4 light years (which is the distance to the nearest star, Proxima Centauri), a method is used which is commonly called the standard candle method. The idea is that if a candle is taken away from me, then the further away it gets, the fainter it appears. If I know how bright the candle actually is, and measure the apparent brightness of the candle when it is far away, then a comparison of those two numbers (and a little mathematics!) gives me the distance. The question for astronomy then was, was there an astronomical standard candle which shone at the same intrinsic brightness wherever it was? Then by measuring its apparent brightness, the distance can be deduced. Harlow Shapely in the 1920s found pulsating stars called cepheids which did just that, and used them to deduce the size of the galaxy.

Among those who cheered Slipher in 1914 was Edwin Hubble. Now with a colleague, Milton Humanson, Hubble used Shapley's technique with the Mount Wilson telescopes in California to determine the distances to galaxies, in particular the Slipher galaxies. In 1929 Hubble presented a paper to the National Academy of Sciences on his findings, perhaps one of the greatest experimental papers of modern astronomy. Under the title 'A Relation Between Distance and Radial Velocity among Extra Galactic Nebulae' he showed that the further away the galaxies were, the faster they were moving away from us.

Does this mean that we are at the centre of everything? In fact all the galaxies are moving away from each other, rather like the expansion of the surface of a balloon.

If you take a balloon, blow it up, mark a number of small 'galaxies' on the surface, and then blow it up some more, you will see all the 'galaxies' move away from each other. This is rather like the expansion of the universe. That is, the universe is expanding, not because the galaxies are moving through space, but because the space between the galaxies is expanding. This type of analogy also helps us to think about the old question of what is the universe expanding into? The question cannot be answered, because it is space itself that is expanding. The four dimensions of our universe, three of space and one of time, can be thought of as the two dimensions of the surface of the balloon. An insect unable to fly, would simply be able to crawl around the surface, never finding an edge or anything 'beyond' the universe.

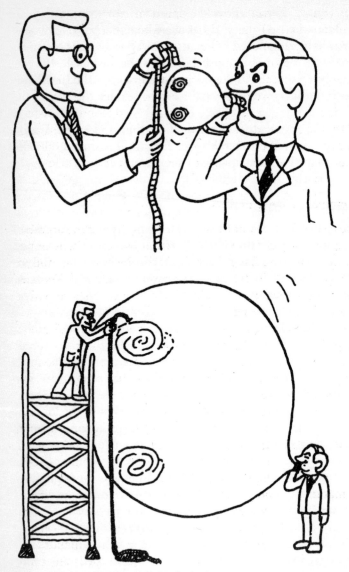

Fig 3.3 *The universe's rate of inflation!*

Of course, if you know the speed of expansion you can calculate when all the galaxies were together; that is when the Big Bang happened. The answer has some uncertainties but you get a figure of about 10–20 billion years. This figure of billions of years is interesting because it is of the same magnitude as figures obtained from the radioactive dating of meteorites, the ages of groups of stars called globular clusters and the decay of radioactive atoms. All these measures of ages do have uncertainties, but all give answers in terms of billions rather than thousands of years for the universe.

An eternal or finite universe?

If the General Theory of Relativity is telling us that the universe is expanding and Hubble's law demonstrated this, is not a beginning in a Big Bang inevitable? The answer is no, and in 1948 physicists Fred Hoyle, Hermann Bondi and Thomas Gold proposed a theory which would give an alternative picture to the Big Bang.

Their motivation was to avoid ours being a 'special time'. If there was a beginning to the universe then by implication, not all times would be the same. Their 'Perfect Cosmological Principle' stated that the laws and properties of the universe should appear the same to all observers at all times. Some cynics have suggested that this was merely a way of English physicists maintaining that there will always be an England!

They accepted that the universe was expanding, but argued that this phenomenon could be better understood in a 'steady state' model of the universe, where there was no beginning but matter was continuously being created throughout space. This new matter, added to the universe at the very small rate of one hydrogen atom per cubic centimetre every 10,000 years, keeps the density of the universe constant as it expands.

The steady state model therefore proposed an ever-expanding universe. It was eternal without beginning or end.

Of course, this has religious implications. One physicist has written, 'The steady state theory is philosophically the most attractive theory because it least resembles the account given in Genesis.' Certainly it has been used against belief in God as Creator, just as the Big Bang has been used for belief. As we shall see, neither type of argument is compelling. The steady state theory still begs the question: why is there a universe rather than nothing, and indeed how did it get into its original expanding state?

However, the overwhelming majority of scientists reject the steady state model, while Hoyle has progressed to a theory of 'little bangs' throughout the universe. The reason why the steady state model has been rejected is not because of religious grounds, but because of observations made in the 1960s. To these we turn next.

An echo of the Big Bang

In the early 1960s, Martin Ryle and his colleagues in Cambridge found that the galaxies which are strong emitters of radio waves are more common the farther one looks back in time. Fully consistent with the Big Bang model, this did not fit the steady state model. However the nail in the coffin of steady state, and the clinching piece of evidence for the Big Bang appeared in 1965.

It was published in a paper with the title 'Infra-red measurement of excess antenna temperature at 4080Mc/s'. Not exactly a title that suggested one of the most exciting discoveries of modern science! Arno Penzias and Robert Wilson were attempting an experiment using microwaves. However, they could not get rid of a static noise which appeared on their instruments. (They even thought it might be due to pigeon droppings and cleaned out their receiver dish!)

They eventually realized that what they had found was the

Fig 3.4 Pigeon droppings or Big Bang relics?

microwave background radiation or 'echo' of the Big Bang. This had been predicted theoretically in the 1940s by George Gamow, Ralph Alpher and Robert Herman. Produced in the Big Bang, it fills the whole of space and has cooled with the expansion of the universe to a temperature of 2.7 K.

The cosmic abundance of helium

The final piece of evidence for the Big Bang concerned the ratio of the amount of hydrogen to helium in the universe. By working backwards from the state of the expanding universe, using appropriate relativistic equations, it is possible to calculate the conditions of pressure and density in the first few moments of the Big Bang. In a classic work in the 1960s Fred Hoyle, with Robert Wagoner and Willy Fowler showed that in the Big Bang model, the universe should start off with 76% hydrogen and 24% helium. Stars create a certain amount of helium but this process is well known and can be easily calculated. In the last decade it has been possible to measure the amount of helium in the universe at present, subtract how much helium has been made by stars and obtain the answer that the universe started off with 24% helium, which is exactly what the Big Bang predicts.

Of course these pieces of evidence cannot prove the Big Bang, but in a sense nothing can. Detectives can only give the best reconstruction of the crime, and they may sometimes get it wrong. The model of the Big Bang is the best model we have at present of how the universe began. Most cosmologists believe that the evidence we see confirms it as a very good picture of what actually happened.

However, although the Big Bang model is almost universally accepted by cosmologists there are still a number of questions which remain unanswered and it is these questions which have proved a growth area of modern research and indeed have provided the motivation for the search for a 'theory of everything'. It is these questions which have made the Big Bang a big business for scientists and theologians alike.

CHAPTER FOUR

THE PROOF OF SCIENCE

Mark Twain once wrote, 'There is something fascinating about science. One gets such a wholesale return of conjecture out of such a trifling investment of fact.'

Such scepticism is rather unusual. The advance of science has been all-conquering. Religious authority within society has been replaced by science, and realms of explanation that were once thought to be the exclusive property of God are now in science's grasp. Whether it be the evolution of the universe, the origin of life, the evolution of species or the emergence of mankind, science has something to say. But more than that. It seems that if we understand the science of everything there is nothing more to say. Technology from the selection of the sex of a baby to a Super Nintendo Game Boy encourages in us the belief that the world is a predictable place, easily manipulated for our own ends.

The world of science is successful in understanding the universe. Its popular image is well summed up by a figure like Mr Spock in *Star Trek*. If we have enough information about the universe, then with logic and a big enough computer we can discover what has happened in the past and what will happen in the future. No problem is large enough to stop science's advance.

Not even the origin of the universe. We have already seen

that the Big Bang model makes sense of our observations of the universe. One or two problems remain, but if we solve them will we then know everything about the universe? Before we make progress on the unanswered questions of the Big Bang, we need to take a short diversion to examine the nature of science and its relationship to the universe.

Many people contrast science with religion in terms that science proves things while religion simply requires dogmatic belief despite the evidence. Such a view is based on a naïve and outdated view of science. It is more of a nineteenth century view of science rather than the reality of the twentieth century.

The nineteenth century gave pride of place to the universe as a mechanism. Newton's laws of motion and gravitation were extremely successful. The world was like a clock, rigid and predictable. Stars hung in fixed space, eternal and unchanging. The universe could be pictured in everyday terms. The motion of the planets could be simulated in the drawing room with a relatively simple clockwork mechanism. This was a deterministic world.

Our everyday experience often reinforces this view. If I am fielding on the boundary at a cricket match, then the motion of the ball through the air from the batsman's shot is predictable. If it were not, then there would be no possibility at all of my attempting to catch it. The force of the bat on the ball and the angle of impact determine where the ball will land.

Such a view of the universe however is not the whole story. General relativity, quantum theory and more recently chaos theory paint quite a different picture.

Understanding the unimaginable

Quantum theory arose from Max Planck's work on electromagnetic radiation from heated bodies, and Albert Einstein's work on the emission of electrons when a metal surface was bathed in ultra-violet radiation. Today, it is one of the most powerful theories of modern physics giving the world lasers, nuclear power, the transistor, and the electron microscope. It has also helped us to understand the conduction of electricity, the structure of the atom, and as we shall see in the next chapter, perhaps the origin of the universe itself.

It is an extremely successful theory of matter on the scale of atoms. The world that it reveals is quite different from the everyday world described by Newton. Instead of things being determined, they are uncertain and uncaused.

This can be illustrated by one of the classic experiments of quantum theory. Imagine a beam of electrons directed at a screen which lights up when an electron hits it. If we put a barrier with two open slits between the source and the screen, a pattern will emerge. It is a pattern of fringes, that is regions of high intensity separated by regions of low intensity in a regular pattern. It is a well known pattern that you see with light in such an experiment. It is called a diffraction pattern and is characteristic of wave motion. If one of the slits is covered, the electrons form a different pattern on the screen grouped around a position corresponding to the centre of the slit.

However, in this experiment, we can control the number of electrons emitted by the source. What happens if we only emit one electron from the source? With one slit closed the electron hits the screen within the one slit pattern. Opening the closed slit, the electron hits the screen within the fringe pattern. But just a moment! If we are talking about one electron then in the two slit experiment it must pass through one of the slits. If that is the case how does it 'know' that the other slit exists so that it falls in the two slit pattern rather than the single slit pattern?

However much one thinks about it, one is drawn to the conclusion that the electron passes through both slits. How can that be? The quantum theory explanation is not to talk

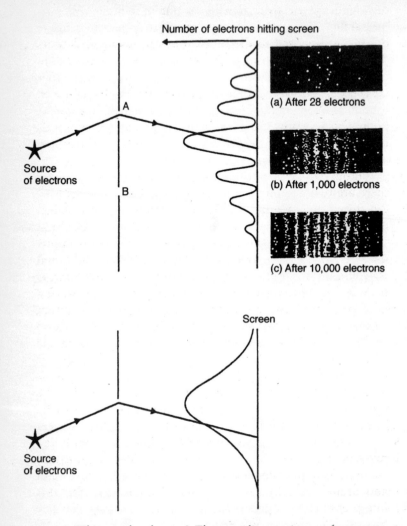

Fig 4.1 Where is the electron? The two slit experiment of quantum theory illustrates its nature. With two slits open you get the characteristic fringe pattern. With one slit open you get a different pattern. How does an electron going through slit A know whether slit B is open or closed?

of where the electron actually is but to talk in terms of probability. You cannot say that the electron passed through one slit as opposed to the other, you can only calculate its probability. Such a situation is impossible to picture in everyday terms, and talk of causes becomes irrelevant. Werner Heisenberg, one of the founders of quantum theory, summed it up in his Uncertainty Principle, which says that you cannot know precisely both the position and the momentum (that is, its velocity multiplied by its mass) of a particle. You can know one or the other precisely but not both.

Although this description of the atomic world is successful there are two main areas of dispute. The first concerns how the uncertain quantum world gives certain answers when interrogated by our macro world, that is the world of television screens and measuring devices. Why, when the electron hits the screen, do we actually know where it is? The traditional answer given by the father of quantum theory, Neils Bohr, is that it is the inter-vention of macro world measuring instruments that 'collapses' the probability of the quantum world into definite answers. The trouble is of course that those very measuring instruments are themselves composed of atoms which have quantum behaviour. What makes them different to atoms or electrons in themselves?

To avoid this difficulty, an alternative is that it is only the intervention of a conscious observer that leads to a measurement. It is not until mind becomes involved that an answer becomes definite. This has the same problem as before, the brain being composed of atoms, but it might be argued that we still do not fully understand the relationship between mind and brain. The physicist John Wheeler has extended this interpretation to suggest that it is in fact mind which has brought the universe into being.

The final suggestion has even more bizarre consequences. Hugh Everett III's 'many worlds' interpretation of quantum theory states that in every act of measurement, each possibility available is realized and at that point the universe splits into separate universes corresponding to the realized possibilities. This means that at this moment in another universe a ten ton polar bear has just landed on another me! Every possibility is realized in different universes. The number of universes that this produces is unimaginable and the majority of physicists have objected to it in terms of it being the antithesis of the quest of physics to look for the simplest explanation. However, it has become popular with cosmologists, particularly those who want to apply quantum theory to the beginning of the universe. This is because the other two interpretations will not work; how can one talk of a measuring device or observer for the whole universe? (The theist may be tempted to provide an answer!)

The second area of dispute is what quantum theory actually tells us about the nature of reality. Some say that the theory is simply a calculational procedure telling us nothing of the actual nature of atoms. Others argue that in fact quantum theory does mean that matter at the atomic level is indeterminate. Heisenberg viewed quantum objects as carrying the potential for such quantities as position and momentum. Quantum theory tells us that at the atomic level our common sense or everyday imagination will not work, but that through mathematics we can understand it.

It is often said that the person who fully understands quantum theory doesn't! The philosophical questions remain unanswered but the success of quantum theory does have profound implications for our view of science, and as we shall see later perhaps for the origin of the universe. It reminds us of the limits of our imagination. To view the world as a rigid clockwork mechanism does not describe the world as it is. It reminds us to be very hesitant to say that something cannot possibly happen. As Bohr remarked, anyone who is not shocked by quantum theory has not understood it.

Quantum theory, surprisingly, has not led to a great deal

of theological speculation, partly perhaps because it is so difficult for the non-mathematician to understand it. Some have argued that the indeterminacy of the quantum world is where free will and God come into the picture. Free will is an expression of the uncertainty in the world, and God acts in the world by directing an electron here or there. Such a view however neglects the fact that quantum effects are only significant at an atomic level. At an everyday level the probabilities are very small. I do have a small probability of being able to walk through a wall, but I am not confident of trying it! A God who works only with electrons at the quantum level will not do a lot.

The same mistake is made by those who argue that quantum theory endorses a view of the world characteristic of the Eastern religions. They stress its subjective nature and a picture of the world more like that of an organism rather than a machine. Now it is true that quantum theory does stress the importance of the observer, and that at an atomic level the rigid machine picture breaks down. However, there are still laws in quantum theory, and at the everyday level quantum effects are small. The situation is a little more subtle and complicated, with both certainty and uncertainty existing together and being dependent on one another.

Simply chaos

When Newton published his great work *Principia* in 1686 it symbolized a view of the world that has survived into popular culture today. His laws of motion and theory of gravitation gave successful descriptions of the motions of planets, moons, comets and even tides. This was a deterministic world, predictable and able to be understood.

If this clockwork universe had been shown not to apply at the atomic level by quantum theory, then does it still apply at an everyday or macro level? Einstein's theory of relativity had already shown its limitations, saying that Newton's laws were only a good approximation for deeper laws where speeds and gravitational fields were small. However, in the last thirty years or so we have become aware of a phenomenon which shows the limitations of Newton's model even more clearly. This phenomenon is called 'chaos' and it makes clear that the world at an everyday level is not as deterministic as we had thought.

In 1961, Ed Lorenz who was a meteorology professor at the Massachusetts Institute of Technology MIT, accidentally came across it. He was interested in air movements in the atmosphere and was trying to model them through mathematical equations and a computer. He would type in the starting conditions, the computer would solve the equations and give a prediction. In one of these computer runs he typed in a number which was just slightly wrong, by only one part in a thousand. His common sense told him that this small error would only cause a very small difference in the final prediction but, much to his surprise, he found that this small error in the starting conditions changed the prediction enormously. What he had come across was a chaotic system.

These systems exhibit a great sensitivity to initial conditions, very different outcomes arising from infinitesimally different starting points. He named the phenomenon 'the butterfly effect': that is, systems like the weather patterns are so sensitive that the flapping of a butterfly's wing in Rio could lead to a hurricane in New York!

The physical laws which determine the weather are well known, and forecasters use these to make weather predictions. Why then do they get things wrong, and why do forecasts get more imprecise the further ahead they predict? Chaos theory explains this by saying that even if the laws are known, the precise predictions are extremely sensitive to the initial conditions. However well the Met Office collects data on pressure and temperature to start off their predictions, there

Fig 4.2 The Nature of Science

will always be a degree of uncertainty. This uncertainty is amplified in a chaotic system. Now this is not to say that gross features like global warming cannot be predicted. It is just to say that precise predictions are impossible.

The importance of chaos therefore is that, in contrast to the 'clockwork world' deduced from Newtonian mechanics, there are systems obeying immutable and precise laws which do not act in predictable and regular ways. When the dynamics of a system are chaotic the outcome can only be predicted if the initial conditions are known to infinite precision. This is obviously impossible as even a computer as large as the universe would not give such precision. This means that for finite beings there is an uncertainty to systems within the everyday world even if the laws of physics are known. It must be stressed that not all systems are chaotic, and for these systems the Newtonian picture is still valid. The planets do orbit the Sun in a regular way.

What chaos theory is saying is that once again the world is a little more subtle than we are often prepared to acknowledge. The consequences of chaos for the evolution of the universe are still being worked out, and only the future will reveal how important it is.

Does this say anything about God? Some will say that this unpredictable nature of certain chaotic systems gives an 'openness' to the world and this is where free will and the actions of God are located. Whether this is the case or not, it must be noted that chaos does not rule out the possibility that an infinitely intelligent being with perfect senses would be able to predict the system.

So what is science?

So far we have looked at some of the great theories of modern physics, namely general relativity, the Big Bang, quantum theory and chaos. Where does this leave us as to the nature of science? It is a question we need to be clear about, especially if we are going to ask where religion fits into the picture.

Science uses observations of the world to look for patterns by which the complexity of the universe can be understood. Most scientists themselves view science in terms of naïve realism. They implicitly believe that theories give an accurate description of the world as it is in itself, so that theories like the Big Bang give a literal description of what actually happened.

The difficulty with such a view is that theories change.

Newton's view of the world as we have seen is revised by general relativity, quantum theory and chaos. It would be foolish to say that the present model of the Big Bang will never change. It is simply the best we have at the moment. Perhaps the often quoted statement that 'Cosmologists are never in doubt, but always in error' needs to be remembered!

From this difficulty, a number of alternative views of science have developed. Positivism sees science as simply telling the story about effects in measuring instruments. Instrumentalism views scientific theories just as calculating devices in order to do things, simply giving us purchase on the world. Finally idealism, stemming from the philosophy of Immanuel Kant, sees science as a function of the way our minds organize the data from our senses. Thus, the order of the physical laws does not exist in nature but is imposed onto nature by our minds. Science does not give us knowledge of the world in itself, rather it shows us how our minds work. To follow an illustration of John Polkinghorne, former Professor of Mathematical Physics at Cambridge, if you fish in an ocean with a net which has four inch holes, it does not mean that when you get your catch you conclude that there are no fish in the ocean smaller than four inches. You have imposed such an order.

Such anti-realist views, that is saying that science does not tell us about the world in itself, have become popular particularly amongst philosophers of science. Obviously the experience that theories do change, the importance of the role of the observer in quantum theory, and the way that social scientists have quite rightly seen the importance of the human in the methodology of science have supported such a view.

However, it must be dismissed. Such a view does not do justice either to the history of science or to the experience of science today. It does not give an adequate explanation for why as a society we spend so much time, effort and money on the scientific enterprise. Why spend fifty million pounds on a telescope which has few technological spin offs if all we are doing is telling a story about how photons of light are received or how our mind works? Psychologists would be much cheaper!

Theories do change but it would be a wrong view of science to think that there is no common ground between successive theories. Einstein's theory must be consistent with Newton at speeds much less than the speed of light. Even major 'revolutions' of theories have an element of continuity, suggesting that we are getting a fuller and more accurate picture of the world.

Idealism in particular has a bad track record! Kant believed that from a consideration of the working of the mind that the universe must always appear to have a particular geometry. The only trouble was that Einstein's geometry is quite different, and is successful in describing the universe.

Finally, scientists know the experience of reality poking its head through our often overly rigid ideas. General relativity, quantum theory and chaos were all in one sense unexpected and initially unimaginable phenomena. There is to science a real feeling of discovery and indeed surprise that often the world is far simpler and more subtle than expected.

In the light of this, if we reject naïve realism and anti-realism, is there another way? Is there a way of holding together the impression of discovery with the acknowledgement of the part played by scientists and the provisional nature of scientific theories? Such a view is called critical realism. It says that science gives us a tightening grip on reality.

It is 'realism' in the sense that it takes seriously what our sense data and scientific instruments do tell us of reality. Science is characterized by what Huxley called 'humility before the facts'.

It is however 'critical' realism for the following reasons. First, it says that our description of reality may not be in naïve everyday terms. We saw this graphically in quantum theory.

Second, it stresses that there is a significant personal role in the method of science. Lorenz in his discovery of chaos had to make personal judgements. Should he spend his time on this particular atmospheric problem in the first place? Should he check why the two predictions were so different or just assume that it was a computer error? These are not trivial questions. Most of us at school will have been asked to do an experiment to obtain some points to be plotted on a graph. We know (from an older pupil's book!) that the points should lie on a straight line, but one of our points is way off. What do we do? Do we say that this point is so significant that the graph is not a straight line, or do we say that this is just a rogue result caused by our attention being distracted as a member of the opposite sex walked by? It is not always easy to say that the only thing to do is to go back and repeat the measurement. For example, that point may have taken valuable time on a telescope and to repeat it you may have to wait six months. There is personal judgement involved. Such judgement is also needed in deciding between two competing theories. Physicists talk of good theories in terms of consistency, unifying power, predictive accuracy, simplicity and elegance. Now the scientific community together limit and reinforce an individual's judgement but the method of science still requires what Michael Polanyi called 'tacit skills' of judgement.

Furthermore, there is a degree of creative imagination in the construction of theories. Einstein's creativity in constructing general relativity was only later checked by experiment. Computers cannot do science.

Third, theories exhibit 'verisimilitude' not absolute truth. They are only partial and provisional ways of describing reality. As more data is gathered, theories will be modified leading us closer to reality.

I suggest that this critical realist view of science is the most true to its nature. It questions the view that science ever gives us a total and finished picture of the world. Arthur C. Clarke noted that if an elderly and distinguished scientist tells you that something is impossible, he is almost certainly wrong! The twentieth century scientist should be a little more hesitant. It also questions the view that science 'proves things'. Science proceeds on the gathering of evidence and then judgements are made on the weighing of that evidence.

Understanding laws

The traditional story that the theory of gravity came from Isaac Newton being hit by a falling apple is very doubtful. It does however stress the earthly nature of the discovery. Newton's friend Edmund Halley then applied the theory to comets and predicted the appearance of a certain comet in the year 1758. Unfortunately, Halley died before the comet appeared (such is science!), but it did appear and was thus named after him.

Halley was assuming that this scientific law proposed by the mind of Newton would apply to these exotic objects called comets. To put it another way he trusted in a resonance between the mathematics of our minds and the mathematics of the universe.

That the universe is intelligible to us is a basic assumption of science. Some historians of science have argued that it is an assumption that stemmed in part from the Christian doctrine of creation. From the perspective of this doctrine, as the universe was freely chosen by God rather than imposed by a system of logic, you had to observe the universe to discover its nature. As God was a God of order you would expect to see laws in the universe, and as humanity was made in the image of God there was the expectation that we could understand that order. Furthermore, monotheism reinforced the assumption that the universe was not under different legislation in different places. There should be a consistency of the laws of physics throughout the universe.

Of course, there were other influences in the development of modern science in the seventeenth century, not least of which was the way the Reformation helped to reject formalized ecclesiastical authority, but it does seem that here was something that Christianity has contributed to science.

Indeed, in this chapter we have discovered that the popular stereotype of the difference between science and religion is outdated. Science does not give a totally impersonal, finalized and deterministic view of the universe. That is not to demean its achievement in describing the universe, but to recognize a necessary humility concerning itself and the value of other perspectives on the world.

CHAPTER FIVE

A SINGULAR PROBLEM
OR TWO?

An old definition of science goes, 'If it moves it's biology, if it smells it's chemistry, and if it doesn't work it's physics!' The Big Bang theory of the origin of the universe does work in explaining many features of the universe, but it still has some unanswered questions. It has received a barrage of criticism from both scientists and religious thinkers. Some of these criticisms have rightly picked up on these unanswered questions, while other criticisms have simply shown an ignorance of the theory itself. We will begin with some of the invalid criticisms and then move on to the unanswered questions. Far from these questions demolishing the theory, we will see that they will lead us into even deeper truths about the universe.

Something out of nothing?

Many people find difficulty in imagining where the matter of the universe comes from to begin with. Surely, they say, there must be an amount of matter or a 'primeval atom' with which to go bang? As Einstein's famous equation $E=mc^2$ implies that energy (E) is equivalent to mass (m) multiplied by the square of the speed of light (c), the question can be translated: where does the energy come from?

Now energy has the property that it can be either positive or negative. Two objects attracted by the force of gravity need energy to pull them apart, and therefore in that state we say that they have negative gravitational energy.

It turns out that the energy in matter in the universe is the same amount as the negative energy in the gravitational field of the universe. Thus the total energy of the universe is zero. In this way you can have something from nothing in terms of the matter in the universe.

Where has all the anti-matter gone?

The existence of anti-matter is not science fiction. The anti-particles of protons and electrons have long been known from the cosmic ray particles entering the Earth's atmosphere, and from experiments in particle accelerators and colliders. Their production within controlled conditions is now a normal part of high energy physics. However, they do not last very long. For example if the anti-particle of an electron, a positron, encounters an electron then the two annihilate with the production of photons of electromagnetic radiation.

Early theories of the Big Bang ran into problems on this particular issue. There seemed to be no reason why the universe should not have started with equal numbers of particles and anti-particles. The trouble is that we see no evidence today of such a significant amount of anti-matter. Subsequent theories suggested that somehow regions of anti-matter were separated from regions of matter. This would mean that some of the galaxies we see in the universe are islands of matter, and others islands of anti-matter. As long as they never meet we would not be able to distinguish between them by light alone. However, such theories have never been successful in suggesting a mechanism able to make this work. The question remains: where has the anti-matter gone?

In the universe there are about two billion photons for every proton. But in order to produce so many photons one billion protons would need to be annihilated with one billion anti-protons. In fact to produce the universe we have today, there must have been a small excess of matter over anti-matter in the ratio of one billion and one protons to one billion anti-protons. This is a remarkable ratio, but it is possible. The 'astonishing' fact that equal amounts of matter and anti-matter were not produced (and thus annihilating each other totally) is now accepted to be due to a small asymmetry in one of the physical theories, the so-called CP non conservation. This predicts that a difference in the decay rates of protons and anti-protons in the early universe is just enough to provide the excess of matter over anti-matter.

In this way all the anti-matter of the universe was annihilated but there was a residue of matter that was left over, and it was from this residue that the universe was made.

The singularity problem

If the above problems have been solved to general satisfaction, we now move on to more disputed problems. The first involves what is known as a singularity. If you take a certain mass and reduce the volume which it is in, then there is an increase in density. As the volume nears zero, so the density nears infinity. Such a state of infinite density is called a singularity, and it is here that the laws of physics break down.

The standard Friedmann models of general relativity suggested that as you traced the universe back in time, it could have begun with a singularity. It is in this context that one of Professor Stephen Hawking's early contributions was made.

Roger Penrose had been working on a solution of Einstein's equations for black holes, investigating whether a singularity must inevitably occur in the collapse of a black hole. Hawking realized that the same equations describing the collapse of a black hole could be turned round to describe the expansion of the universe out of a singularity. In one sense the universe is a time-reversed black hole. Penrose and Hawking showed that if gravity was attractive, if the universe was expanding and if time travel was impossible then general relativity required that space and time must come to a singularity in the past.

So the standard model of the hot Big Bang describes the origin of the universe as an expansion from a singularity, that is a point of infinite density, some 15 billion years ago. However, such a model raises immediate problems. General relativity has the unusual property of predicting that there can arise states in which its jurisdiction does not apply. That is, it predicts that it cannot predict. As we have seen, general relativity suggests that time is not completely independent of space, and that gravity is then explained as a consequence of this space-time being curved by the distribution of mass-energy in it. Thus the distribution of mass determines the geometry of space and the rate of flow of time. This raises two problems.

First, at a singularity there is infinite density and infinite curvature of space-time. General relativity is unable to cope with this infinity and predicts its own downfall, that is, the theory breaks down at the singularity. Second, general relativity as a theory is inconsistent with quantum theory. General relativity, which is extremely successful in describing the large scale structure of the universe needs to specify mass and its position in order to then describe the geometry and rate of flow of time. At a singularity where the gravitational field is so strong, and the whole universe is so small that it is on the atomic scale of quantum theory, it is believed that quantum effects should be important. Quantum theory, however, says that you can never know both the mass and position without an intrinsic uncertainty. You cannot have both general relativity and quantum theory to describe a situation.

The singularity problem therefore is that general relativity is unable to give a description of the singularity, or in other words, the initial conditions of the expansion of the universe. To put it another way, present scientific theories are unable to predict what will come out of the singularity. They can describe the subsequent expansion but are unable to reach back beyond an age of 10^{-43} seconds to zero. Hawking commented on the singularity problem that God does play dice and sometimes he throws them where they cannot be seen! This 'limit' of scientific theory, unable to reach back to the very beginning, was frustrating to physicists but attractive to some theologians. Former NASA astrophysicist Robert Jastrow captures the mood:

> For the scientist who has lived by his faith in the power of reason, the story ends like a bad dream. He has scaled the mountains of ignorance; he is about to conquer the highest peak; and as he pulls himself over the final rock, he is greeted by a band of theologians who have been sitting there for centuries.[9]

The question for some in the light of this is whether God is needed to 'fix' the initial conditions of the universe.

The fine-tuning problem

The second major unanswered question for the Big Bang model is how the universe comes to be so finely tuned in so many respects. What do we mean by this?

First of all, the universe on the basis of the microwave background radiation is extremely smooth on a large scale. Recent results from the COBE satellite suggest that the temperature of the microwave background varies across the whole sky by less than one part in 30,000. How does this come about, especially for regions which have not been in causal contact? That is, in winding our model back to when the microwave background was produced we find that regions that are today at exactly the same temperature are separated by a distance which is greater than that which could have been covered by information travelling at the maximum speed, the speed of light. How did one region know what temperature the other region was to match its temperature so exactly? Did the universe have to start off in such a uniform condition?

Second, why is it that the universe is so near the critical rate of expansion? To see what this means imagine you had a machine which made universes.

On this machine you would have two dials. One dial would control the expansion force of the Big Bang. The other would control gravity, the force which pulls everything back together. Set the dials to whatever you wanted and out would come a universe. The trouble is you would find it to be a very boring experiment! After a few billion attempts, you would begin to realize that in order to get a universe which would produce carbon-based life those two dials need to be set quite precisely. If you get the gravitational force too high, then the universe would appear but within a microsecond, gravity would pull everything back together into the opposite of a Big Bang, a Big Crunch! If you get the expansion rate too high, then the universe would expand at such a rate that gravity would be unable to form stars and galaxies. In fact in order to get structure within the universe these dials need to be balanced to within 1 part in 10^{60} (1 followed by 60 zeros). In Paul Davies' words, that is the same accuracy as shooting at a target one centimetre square on the other side of the universe—and hitting it! Why is it that early in the expansion, the expansion force of the Big Bang was balanced so carefully with the gravitational force?

Third, what is the origin of galaxies? Galaxies form by gravity-amplifying density fluctuations in the universe. After

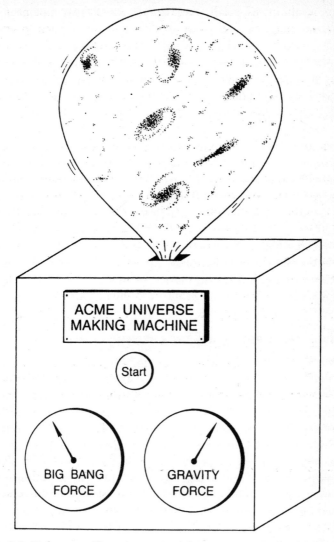

Fig 5.1 *Make yourself a universe! In order to get structure and carbon-based life in the universe the two dials need to be balanced to 1 part in* 10^{60}.

two years of observing the universe, the COBE satellite has recently found evidence for such density fluctuations or ripples in the microwave background. These ripples could be the embryos of superclusters of galaxies. They give evidence of clouds some 500 million light years across when the universe was only 300,000 years old. But where did the density fluctuations come from, what determines their size and how do they grow?

Gravity works on the density fluctuations, very quickly building them into stars and galaxies, but in an expanding universe this process is slowed. To overcome this has developed the proposal of cold dark matter, that is vast amounts of unseen exotic particles, acting as the 'seeds' of galaxy formation. This proposal looks very promising but even this model has been called into question very recently due to observations that the distribution of galaxies itself is like a sponge, exhibiting holes and walls. At present there is no generally accepted solution to the problem of galaxy formation.

Anthropic principles and many universes

One possible answer to the fine-tuning problem is that if the universe was spatially infinite (or there were infinitely many universes), we could be living in a region that by chance was smooth and regular with the initial state chosen randomly. We see a smooth and regular universe because it is selected by the fact that it must be consistent with our existence. In a chaotic region we would not exist in it to observe it. This proposal comes under what has been called the anthropic principle. Out of the multitude of universes we 'select' a fine-tuned universe, because if it was not fine-tuned we would not exist to see it!

It is important to note that in order to provide an explanation, the anthropic principle needs to be held with a theory of many universes.

There have been many proposals for such a theory. One is to say that our visible universe is only one small part of an infinite universe. Elsewhere the laws of physics are all slightly different. Another claims that the mass of the universe is so great that eventually gravity will reverse the expansion bringing the universe back to a Big Crunch. Some then say that the universe 'bounces' back into a Big Bang and the process of this oscillating universe goes on into infinity, thus providing an infinite number of universes. At each 'bounce' the parameters change leading to different universes. The obvious difficulty with this is at one such bounce there is no reason to rule out the possibility that the parameters could change in such a way so that gravity does not reverse the expansion. Then the universe would expand for ever, and there would be no other universes in the future! As we have already seen there is also the bizarre suggestion of Everett's interpretation of quantum theory which says that whenever a measurement is made of the quantum world the universe fulfils all quantum possibilities forming a new universe with each possibility. This leads to literally billions and billions of independent universes all slightly different to each other.

However, this coupling of the anthropic principle with a theory of many universes is more of a metaphysical suggestion than a physical theory. The question must be asked: in what sense do other universes exist if they have no observable consequences? The trouble with these theories of many universes is, just how do you pass information from one universe to another in order to know that it is there? There are many who argue with some justification that talk of many universes goes beyond physics, to the extent that it becomes an explanation of the way the world is on the same level as religious explanations.

How do we assess the anthropic principle? It sounds a necessary cautious word that our observation of the universe is dependent on the fact that we are here. However, as an

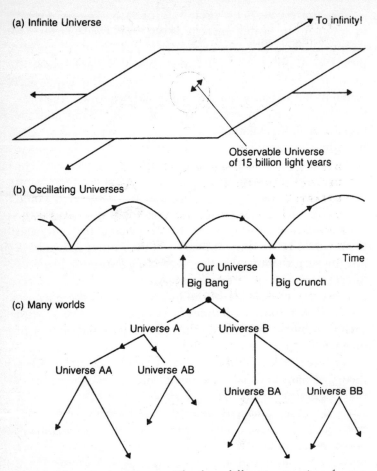

(a) Infinite Universe

To infinity!

Observable Universe
of 15 billion light years

(b) Oscillating Universes

Time

Our Universe
Big Bang

Big Crunch

(c) Many worlds

Universe A   Universe B

Universe AA   Universe AB

Universe BA   Universe BB

Fig 5.2 Many, many universes. The three different suggestions for our universe being only one of many.
(a) Our universe is only a small part of an infinite universe.
(b) There have been expanding and collapsing universes before ours, and there will be many after ours.
(c) Everett's many worlds interpretation of quantum theory that says the universe splits to form new universes whenever a quantum measurement is taken.

explanation of fine-tuning it has the difficulty of being potentially too successful. If you have so many universes then you can explain literally everything without recourse to understanding the physics. You simply say in the case of any phenomenon that it is just like that because we are here. Furthermore, Hawking has raised the objection of why there are so many other galaxies when only one would be sufficient for life to exist? Indeed it can be argued that life is more probable in a universe with only one star, rather than one with lots of galaxies.

Inflation

An alternative possibility to explain the fine-tuning problem is the attempt to show that quite a number of different initial configurations would have evolved to produce a universe like the one we observe.

Chaotic cosmology attempted to show that whatever the initial conditions, frictional processes within the universe would produce a smooth universe, rather like the action of the tide in smoothing away footprints on the sand.

These theories were unsuccessful, but in 1980 Alan Guth proposed a model called inflation. These inflationary models of the early universe postulate an early rapid (exponential) expansion, between 10^{-35} and 10^{-33} seconds due to a phase change leading to the introduction of various particles into the universe with the effect of anti-gravity. Guth discovered this while examining how the fundamental forces could be unified into a single force. At high energies in the early universe, it is thought that the forces are unified but as the universe cools, one of the forces (the strong force which is responsible for the structure of the nuclei of atoms) becomes distinct from the others. This has the effect of a phase change. This releases energy into the universe, in a similar way the phase change of steam into water releases energy in scalding.

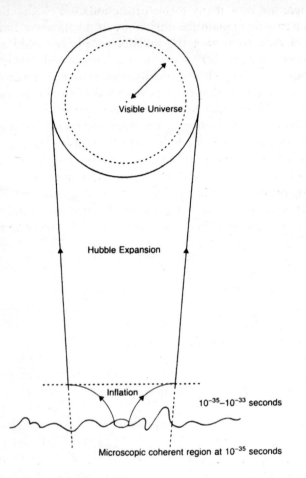

Fig 5.3 The inflationary model. From our present-day expanding universe we can extrapolate back in time assuming a normal Hubble-type expansion. The problem is that at early times we cannot explain how widely separated regions look the same. Inflation between 10^{-35} seconds and 10^{-33} seconds gives the universe an accelerated, exponential expansion. This reduces the size of region needed to form our present-day universe.

There are now many forms of the inflation model, but it does naturally explain the uniformity of the universe and the rate of expansion after the inflationary phase would automatically become very close to the critical value without assuming carefully chosen initial conditions. The significance of these models is that they mean that the initial state of the universe did not have to be chosen with great care.

However, even if inflation is correct (and there is no general agreement on this at the moment) it cannot be the case that every initial configuration would have led to a universe similar to the one we observe. Indeed, even if inflation solves the fine-tuning problem we are still left with the singularity problem, the frustration of not being able to describe the initial state of the universe. It is here that the work of Professor Stephen Hawking becomes important.

CHAPTER SIX

THE UNCERTAINTY OF QUANTUM GRAVITY

The belief that science will ultimately answer every question has long been an implicit assumption of modern physics. The success and power of physical theories such as quantum theory and general relativity to describe such a diverse range of physical phenomena from the structure of atoms to the structure of black holes has been quite astonishing. This has led to the possibility of a theory of everything, that is one physical theory which will unite all previous theories and describe the very beginning of the universe.

The aim of Stephen Hawking is for a complete description of the universe by means of such a single theory. This theory would describe not only how the universe changes with time but also the initial conditions or starting point of the universe. Physics works on an everyday distinction between evolutionary laws and initial conditions. If I hit a golf shot, it is the law of gravity which tells me how the ball will move through the air. However, that is not sufficient by itself to tell me where the ball will land. To predict its path I need to know what speed it was given at the impact of the club, and also the angle of the club face. The law of gravity will not tell me the initial conditions, they have to be specified separately.

In the same way, if we only have the laws which determine

the evolution of the universe, we still need the initial conditions to determine its shape, size, temperature and composition. Some like Hoyle in his steady state model have attempted to avoid having to specify the initial conditions by saying that the universe has always existed. Alternatively, inflationary models suggest that the universe is not dependent at all on initial conditions. If I pour a liquid into a jar from a variety of heights I know that after some sloshing around it will settle down to the same level in the jar. Such a view is frustrating to many scientists because it would mean that the initial conditions can never be known. However, it does not work for all possible initial conditions. If I go too high to pour the liquid, it might splash out, or even miss the jar altogether!

There are some who would even say that initial conditions are beyond physics itself and are purely the domain of religion. Perhaps God sets up the universe with special initial conditions, which are outside the domain of science to explain. We shall have more to say about this in the next chapter.

However, none of these alternatives appeal to Hawking. He wants a theory to describe the initial conditions. At the heart of such a theory is a unification of two of the great theories of modern physics, general relativity and quantum theory. General relativity describes the force of gravity, while quantum theory describes matter on the atomic scale. The result of combining these two theories would be a quantum theory of gravity.

Black holes ain't so black

Hawking's work on uniting gravity and quantum theory arises from his earlier work on black holes. He showed that in the early expanding universe, the high temperatures and pressures would give rise to low mass black holes, objects within which singularities also occurred. At these singularities, the laws of physics would break down in the same way that they break down at a singularity at the beginning of the universe.

In the early 1970s, Hawking proposed that the surface area of a black hole can never decrease. Entropy, the measure of disorder within a closed system also never decreases. He likened the surface area of a black hole to entropy but clearly said that it was not an actual measure of entropy. If it was a measure of entropy, then this would imply that it had a temperature and would emit radiation, which to Hawking's mind was unthinkable.

However, Jacob Bekenstein, a Californian research student did think about it, and suggested that black holes did indeed have entropy and temperature. Initially, Hawking resisted this, but late in 1973 he changed his mind, and by bringing quantum theory into the picture he found that black holes do emit radiation. In February 1974, at a meeting in the Rutherford Appleton Laboratory near Oxford, he announced what has been called one of the greatest achievements of the past fifty years of physics.

According to quantum theory effects, these objects should emit X-rays and gamma rays and this acts as a kind of evaporation which leads to the removal of these black holes and their singularities. In Hawking's words 'black holes ain't so black'. This is important as it is the first example of a prediction that depended in an essential way on both general relativity and quantum theory. Could it also mean that quantum theory might be able to remove the singularities predicted by general relativity? It is this work that encourages Hawking to pursue more speculative ideas concerning the origin of the universe.

A quantum theory of gravity

A quantum theory of gravity would answer the singularity and the fine-tuning problems by a principle, a 'theory of everything', that picked out one initial state and hence one model of the universe. The only trouble is, how do you get such a theory? How do you reconcile quantum theory and general relativity and how do you apply quantum theory to the universe?

While acknowledging that a complete and consistent combination of quantum theory and gravity has not been achieved, Hawking nevertheless believes that some of its features are fairly certain. One feature he proposes, in order to describe the universe by quantum theory, is that the calculations be done using imaginary time, that is its time scale is based on the square root of minus one. The calculations would then use what is termed Euclidean space-time, where any distinction between time and space disappears.

This has the following important implication. Imagine the surface of a sphere. It is finite in size (you need a certain amount of paint to paint it), but there is no edge or boundary to its surface. This same property of a finite size with no boundaries is possible in four dimensions of space, rather than the two dimensions of the surface of a sphere. But the universe as we know it has three dimensions of space and one dimension of time. Hawking's proposal is that when the universe is the size of the quantum scale, the ordinary concept of time is transcended and becomes like another dimension of space, thus giving the universe four dimensions of space. This in fact is a well known device used elsewhere in quantum theory. As the universe expands and grows larger than the quantum scale, so time crystallizes out into a dimension distinct from space. It is important to stress that the use of imaginary time and hence Euclidean space-time is a mathematical device to calculate answers about real time.

The second proposed feature of a quantum theory of gravity is that gravity is indeed represented by curved space-time. If the universe's space-time stretches back to infinity (that is, the universe has no beginning in real time) or it starts with a singularity, the problem remains of specifying the initial conditions.

However, using Euclidean space-time there is a third possibility:

> It is possible for space-time to be finite in extent and yet have no singularities . . . at which the laws of science broke down and no edge of space-time at which one would have to appeal to God or some new law to set the boundary conditions of space-time.[10]

That is, space-time is seen like the surface of a sphere, finite and yet without a boundary.

Now what does this mean? If, as in this proposal, time becomes a superficial feature of nature, then as we go back in the history of the universe we approach but never reach time zero. Time has faded away before we reach a time zero singularity. The universe has a finite past of 15 billion years, but no beginning in time with no temporal edge or boundary. It has been likened to the edge of a frayed sweater. The smooth surface turns into a tangle of unravelling threads but where does the 'fray' begin?

Hawking's quantum theory of gravity therefore suggests that there would be no singularity of the Big Bang at which the laws of science would break down. In real time, some 15 billion years ago, the universe would have a minimum size corresponding to the universe having arisen by a chance quantum fluctuation from a state of absolutely nothing to a small, finite expanding state.

Quantum theory deals with events which do not have deterministic causes. By applying quantum theory to the universe, Hawking is saying that the event that triggered the Big Bang did not have a cause. In this way, science is able not only to encompass the laws of evolution but also the initial conditions.

To summarize, Hawking has proposed that first, quantum theory needs to be applied to the universe; second, in this the time dimension will become a dimension of space; and

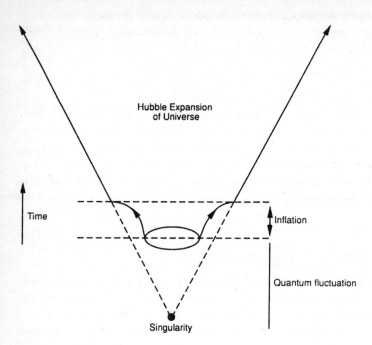

Fig 6.1 Hawking's universe. Instead of the universe beginning at a singularity as would be expected by extrapolating the Hubble expansion back in time, the universe arises from a quantum fluctuation as an already finite, expanding region which is then amplified by inflation.

third, there exists a no boundary proposal. It should be noted that these proposals were originally suggested by Hawking and Jim Hartle largely for aesthetic reasons. The result is that you avoid the problem of the laws of physics breaking down at a singularity. Thus the initial condition which Hawking proposes amounts to saying that there is no boundary where initial conditions have to be specified.

This 'no boundary' condition with a model of inflation, Hawking argues, would naturally explain various aspects of the universe. First, the beginning of time would be a regular, smooth point of space-time and the universe begins its expansion in a smooth and ordered state thus explaining the large scale uniformity. Secondly, the universe began with the minimum possible non-uniformity allowed by the uncertainty principle. Inflation would amplify these non-uniformities leading to structures such as galaxies.

Hawking examines the possibilities of string theories, which are recent developments in trying to unify the forces of nature, uniting gravity and quantum mechanics into a complete unified theory. These theories still have severe problems but he has the faith to think that a complete unified theory is possible within this generation.

A theory of not so everything?

What is the status of Hawking's theory of everything? Is it generally accepted in the scientific community, does it rest on firm foundations, and does it in fact explain everything?

It needs to be stressed that Hawking's views on quantum gravity are speculative, that is, they are not widely accepted. Indeed there exist other suggestions quite different to Hawking's which attempt to answer the same problems of initial conditions. Hawking's former collaborator, Professor Roger Penrose, argues for a different theory based on gravitational entropy. The lack of consensus in the scientific community should make us cautious about accepting any one theory at the present time.

In addition, it is not clear whether some things will work, even to the extent of whether quantum theory can be legitimately applied to the whole universe. With the possibilities of so-called string theories uniting gravity and quantum theory still having severe problems, Hawking himself admits that a consistent theory of quantum gravity is not yet available. What he does is to say, 'If I did have a consistent theory it would look something like this.' One should be cautious with such an approach.

Barrow[11] discusses the question of singularities at some length and concludes that until we better understand the nature of time we will not know whether the no boundary ideas are correct. Gingerich[12] and Tipler[13] go even further, criticizing Hawking's 'sleight of hand', noting that the no boundary condition simply replaces the classical singularity by a quantum singularity. (That is, the four dimensional sphere of zero radius forms a boundary condition to Hawking's universe.) Thus the no boundary condition is not fully implemented.

It is not clear that the no boundary condition with inflation will solve the galaxy formation problem and there is the more fundamental problem, which Hawking again admits, that such a model may be too mathematically complicated for exact predictions to be calculated.

Finally, such a 'theory of everything', even if free from scientific difficulties, still leaves questions unanswered. Polkinghorne and Professor Russell Stannard[14] rightly point out that Hawking has still to 'smuggle in' the requirement that the universe must have gravity and quantum behaviour. Why was it that the laws of quantum theory governed the process?

It is perhaps instructive to hear the views of one of the other leading cosmologists in the world, John Barrow, who is Professor of Astronomy at Sussex University. In his 1988 Gifford Lectures at the University of Glasgow, he argued that the structure of the universe is not determined or 'understood' when we know all the laws of nature. A theory of everything is necessary but insufficient for a full explanation of the universe we observe. He suggests that such a theory must be complemented by many other things. If Hawking's no boundary proposal proves to be incorrect, then we are back to finding some way of specifying initial conditions. Then, what is the origin of the laws of physics and the physical constants? These constants determine the strength of forces, and even if a theory of everything was to somehow specify them, other theories of the early universe say that these constants could be randomly changed. Then to specify our universe you would also have to have knowledge of symmetry breakings, anthropic selection effects and categories of thought. Barrow uses the analogy of Newton's laws and the motion of the planets. Newton's laws do not tell us the number of planets or their direction of rotation. These need to be added to the laws to fully describe the solar system.

Hawking may be proceeding along the right lines in formulating a possible theory of the beginning of the universe. But a so-called theory of everything does not explain everything. This together with the scientific question marks put against Hawking's particular theory, should warn us to be cautious about any view which suggests that *A Brief History of Time* answers all the questions. If that is true in the area of science, it is even more important in the area of God.

CHAPTER SEVEN

TO PROVE OR NOT TO PROVE GOD, THAT IS THE QUESTION

Many Christian apologists welcomed the Big Bang theory of the origin of the universe with open arms. After all, they argued, if the universe started with an explosion, then who lit the blue touch paper? Is not God required to start the whole thing off? Edward Milne, Professor of Mathematics at Oxford, concluded his work on the expansion of the universe by saying, 'The first cause of the universe is left for the reader to insert. But our picture is incomplete without him.' Is this a valid type of argument and what does a theory of everything have to say to it?

Who caused it?

Within theology this first cause argument comes under the title of the Cosmological Argument for the existence of God. Its history can be traced to Aristotle in the fourth century BC, but its chief proponent was Thomas Aquinas in the thirteenth century AD. Aquinas gave 'Five Ways' of arguing for the existence of God, of which the second way involved the argument from cause. He argued that nothing can cause itself and so it is possible to go back in a series of causes to a First Cause, and this is God. In present day terms, the universe can

Fig 7.1 A Master Mind?

be traced back through a series of causes to the Big Bang, and the cause of this is God.

The Big Bang theory itself has highlighted this argument in our own day, and it has been equally popular from pubs to Popes. Perhaps the imagery of the Big Bang being a form of explosion of pre-existing material has reinforced the view. Modern philosophers and theologians have seen an argument that seemed dead now having a glimmer of life. Some tend to think that science will never-be able to get over the singularity problem, and in Jastrow's image this summit is only for religion. Richard Swinburne has argued that the universe is brought about by God on the basis that this provides a 'simpler beginning of explanation' than does the theory of an un-caused universe.

This is a difficult argument, unfortunately often born from an ignorance of science. However, even before the arrival of Hawking, many criticisms had been levelled at the argument.

A limited cause?

There are three main philosophical problems with this argument from cause and effect.

First, surely the whole framework of cause and effect only applies within the universe. Immanuel Kant suggested that cause and effect is only to do with the way our minds deal with the data of the world. As was argued in Chapter 4, Kant's philosophy is not convincing, but it does remind us that all our knowledge of cause and effect is from within this universe. To speak of causes in some way beyond this universe is highly questionable.

In addition, Einstein's general relativity theory implies that time is very much part of the physical universe. As the theologian Augustine had stated much earlier, the universe is not created in time but with time. To ask what caused something assumes a framework of time, but there is no such framework beyond the universe!

Second, the philosophers David Hume and Bertrand Russell pointed out that it is wrong to move from saying that every event in the universe has a cause, to the statement that the whole universe has a cause. You can say that every human being has a mother, but you cannot say that the human race as a whole has a mother. To put it another way, causation only applies to changes in things, not to existence itself.

Third, if we ask what caused the universe, then should we not ask what caused God? 'Who made God?' is a very popular question! The story goes of a theologian who when asked what God was doing before he made the universe replied, 'He was making hell for people who ask questions like that!' Such questions however cannot be taken lightly. If we refuse to ask the question of what caused God, can we deny others the right to refuse to ask what caused the universe? Why should God be self-explanatory when the universe is not?

We might say (correctly in fact) that to ask 'who made God' assumes a temporal framework beyond the universe which is invalid. It is rather like asking how many corners a circle has. It sounds like a valid question but there is no answer. But in saying this, we are simply acknowledging the first criticism, and so our cause and effect argument is undermined.

God and quantum gravity?

It is said that when Laplace presented his 4,000 page mathematical work on celestial motions to Napoleon, he was asked, 'M. Laplace, they tell me that you have written this large book on the system of the universe, and have never even mentioned its Creator'. Laplace replied, 'Sir, I have no need of that hypothesis'.

Laplace was reacting against Newton who invoked the hypothesis of God to stop the universe collapsing in on itself. God was in Charles Coulson's words 'a God of the gaps'. If science cannot explain it, then insert God into the gap of knowledge. The only trouble was that as science explained more and more so God was pushed out of the gap.

Hawking's theological motivation seems to be a reaction to an audience with the Pope during the 1981 Vatican conference on cosmology. He writes: 'He told us that . . . we should not inquire into the big bang itself because that was the moment of Creation and therefore the work of God'.[15]

It is clear that Hawking profoundly disagrees with this 'god of the gaps' attitude, even to the extent of possibly seeing himself as a latter day Galileo. In fact, Tipler[16] has pointed out that the published version of the Pope's address on that occasion is quite different to that which Hawking reports, and did not presume to set limits to scientific inquiry about the initial singularity, but argued that science was unable to answer the question of why the universe exists at all.

Nevertheless, Hawking believes his 'theory of everything' has profound theological implications. He states:

> Most people believe that God allows the universe to evolve according to a set of laws and does not intervene in the universe to break these laws . . . but it would still be up to God to wind up the clockwork and choose how to start it off. So long as the universe had a beginning, we could suppose it had a Creator.[17]

If the no boundary proposal is correct, God had no freedom at all to choose initial conditions and: 'The universe would have neither beginning nor end: it would simply be. What place, then, for a Creator?'[18]

Here Hawking is rejecting God's role as creator in the sense of an efficient cause starting off the universe in time.

The challenge of a theory of everything, to put it simply, is that the blue touch paper could have lit itself. Who then needs God? Through a unified theory which specifies the initial conditions such a Creator becomes irrelevant. God is not required to light the blue touch paper of the Big Bang: it does that for itself.

The argument therefore for a first cause to the universe becomes irrelevant. Quantum theory tells us that events do not have causes at the quantum level. If as in quantum gravity, this is applied to the universe, then the universe as an event, even if it is finite in age does not require a first cause. Some writers have attacked Hawking without really grasping this. They argue from such things as an increasing amount of disorder in the universe that the universe is not eternal but has a beginning. They then make the jump to say that beginning implies cause. Hawking is still allowing the universe to be finite in age, but he is saying that you can have beginning without cause. To put it another way, if time only crystallizes out later in the history of the universe, then you cannot apply cause/effect arguments at all in its beginning.

Does this just about wrap it up for God?

In the light of this undermining of the cosmological argument both in the logic of philosophy and in a physical theory which does away with a cause of the universe, we might be tempted to agree with *The Hitchhiker's Guide to the Galaxy* in saying, 'that about wraps it up for God'!

Hawking's picture in many ways is extremely attractive. It simultaneously attempts to solve the singularity and fine-tuning problems through a unification of the fundamental theories of modern physics. It allows scientists to reach the mountain top without the help of theologians.

He sees the universe as being intelligible and at a fundamental level having an inner unity. These are things that the Christian faith would affirm and indeed locate in a Creator God. His picture of the origin of the universe helps us to see the fallacy of a 'god of the gaps' argument for the existence of God. To argue in such a way always risks God being pushed out of the gap by science and becoming irrelevant. That 'final' gap of the initial conditions of the universe, if not filled in by Hawking's theory of quantum gravity, is at least within reach. Therefore we need to be very cautious in arguing for the existence of God in this way.

If Hawking is to be welcomed for these things, we need to be careful not to go too far. We have seen that severe scientific difficulties and lack of general agreement remain concerning this theory. In addition far from being a 'theory of everything', there are many aspects of the universe which lie outside the theory.

If the theory reminds us that we cannot prove God by the cosmological argument, it certainly does not disprove the existence of God. Although the popular view of Hawking's work has often been to see it as an attack on God, it is far from that. There are a number of things about Hawking's views on God which need to be clearly noted.

First, he takes as an assumption without justification that the universe is intelligible to us, that is we are free to observe it and describe it in mathematical terms. However, this is surely an aspect of the universe which needs explanation. John Polkinghorne was Professor of Mathematical Physics at Cambridge where he encountered first hand the intelligibility of the world in the area of particle physics. Now an ordained minister in the Church of England, he argues that it is a striking and non-trivial fact that the pattern of mathematics is realized in the physical structure of the world and that our minds are able to solve problems that the physical world presents. In the light of this assumption of intelligibility used by science, Polkinghorne suggests that the most reasonable explanation is the existence of a Creator who is the common ground of the rationality of our minds and the universe. We may add that a mathematical account of the creation of the universe implicitly assumes that the mathematical laws are transcendent, that is that they are not contained by the physical universe. Yet where do these laws come from? Is the most reasonable explanation once again a rational Creator?

Second, Hawking tends to identify God as exclusively a 'deistic' Creator, making God vulnerable to being pushed out of the gaps. Deism viewed God as the initiator or originator of the universe, but that was all. It was as if God lit the blue touch paper and then went off for a cup of tea to have nothing more to do with the universe. Little consideration was given to historical revelation or religious experience which may point to God as sustainer and law-giver of the universe. Hawking talks of God in much the same way and so his work is an attack on deism, rather than Christian theism.

Third, this is a popular 'conflict' approach to the relationship between scientific and theological description, that is both descriptions say the same kind of things about the same thing. It means that the existence of a scientific description of an event invalidates its consideration as God's creative activity. There is no concept of the complementary nature of scientific and religious descriptions which would allow a totally naturalistic account of creation but not see this as ruling out a providential account. Such an approach would agree with Hawking and advocate a scientific explanation of the origin of the universe without the hypothesis of a God of the gaps. However, this approach would say that such an explanation is not complete in itself.

It is an approach which has been championed in recent years by the late Donald Mackay, Professor of Neuroscience at Keele. In his view scientific and biblical statements can be different, but both true, because they represent different but complementary aspects of one larger reality.

The fact that two statements can be different but both true is not sometimes easily grasped, yet is basic to everyday life. For example you may define a 'kiss' as 'the approach of two pairs of lips, the reciprocal transmission of carbon dioxide and microbes, and the juxtaposition of two orbicular muscles in a state of contraction'. Now that is a true definition of a kiss. But if I go to my wife and say, 'My darling, I would love to get together with you for a reciprocal transmission of carbon dioxide and microbes, and a contraction of orbicular muscles', I know what the answer would be, and in no uncertain terms! In that context, one is not too concerned with the scientific description, but more concerned with questions of purpose and value. The kiss is better described by the purpose behind it, in terms of the love between two

Fig 7.2 Conflicting or Complementary?

people. Now that is a very different description. Which one is a true definition of a kiss? They are different, but both are true. Indeed, you require both for a full understanding of a kiss.

Another way of putting it is to talk of the old distinction between 'how' and 'why' questions. Of course, this distinction in terms of language is not simple. However, it is helpful to understand that science is primarily concerned about 'how' questions. How did the universe arise out of a Big Bang? How do gas clouds collapse under gravity to form stars? It is a successful discipline because it limits itself to these kinds of questions. To note that it does not address 'why' questions is not to introduce a god of the gaps but simply to recognize that science is not about value and purpose.

In this way it is possible to affirm with Hawking the origin of the universe being a fluctuation in a quantum field but at the same time hold a complementary affirmation that the universe owes its existence to the sovereign will of God.

In fact it seems that Hawking himself sees such a point. At the very end of his book, he rounds on philosophers who spend their time on linguistic analysis rather than addressing the question 'why should there be a universe at all?' The question of 'why is there something rather than nothing' is an old question of philosophy. In 1710 Leibnitz discussed it in his 'Principle of Sufficient Reason' which stated that there must be a full and complete explanation for everything that exists. Therefore the ultimate explanation of the universe must lie outside itself. It must lie in a being that is self-explanatory.

Now such an argument cannot logically prove the existence of God. Some, like the atheist Bertrand Russell simply refused to ask the 'why' question at all. Why should there be a reason? Others ask why should a God be self-explanatory when the universe is not?

However, for some people the consideration of the 'why' question may be a pointer towards God. Science, here at the limit of its arena of enquiry, raises the religious questions. Where do the laws of physics, including a 'theory of everything' come from? Why are they intelligible to us? Why is there a universe for such laws to describe, and what is its purpose? Quantum gravity leaves these questions unanswered. Science has raised the questions, but their answers lie beyond its own domain.

In reply to criticism of an earlier form of *A Brief History of Time*, Hawking wrote, 'I thought I had left the question of the existence of a supreme being completely open. . . . It would be perfectly consistent with all we know to say that there was a being responsible for the laws of physics.'[19]

The question of God, even it seems for Hawking, is still open. A theory of everything does not rule out God. Nor does it prove God. The 'why' question may be a pointer to God but it is not a proof. So is there any way to get to God? Is there anything about the universe that would lead us to its designer? It is to this question that we turn next.

CHAPTER EIGHT

A DESIGNER WAY TO GOD?

What have the age and size of the observable universe, nuclear energy levels in beryllium and carbon, the remarkable properties of water and the amount of oxygen in the atmosphere have in common? All these things are essential to the existence of carbon-based life and are determined by subtle balances among the forces of nature. These balances have led to a remarkable phenomenon of the last two decades: many scientists, in studying the origin of the universe, cannot leave God alone. This is not just because many scientists are in fact believing Christians, it is that the nature of the universe itself seems to raise the 'God' question.

Science seems to be raising questions which it itself is unable to answer. We have already considered the question of why there is a universe rather than nothing. Now we encounter the question: why is the universe the way it is? This does not mean that science will not be able to explain how the universe came from a Big Bang or how these balances in the universe come about. But that does not take away the question: why is the universe this way?

Design or not design?

The nature of the universe has often raised these types of questions in history. In their broadest sense they have existed

Fig 8.1 An original design?

at least since the Middle Ages but elements of them can be traced back to the Greeks and some would argue to the Hebrew scriptures. Certainly the creation narratives in Genesis, the wisdom literature and even the prophetic writings reflect a belief in the orderly and providential design of the world.

This popular theistic argument, called the design argument, occurs in philosophy from the time of Anaxagoras in 500BC onwards. It attempts to move from the orderly and apparently designed character of the world to a designer. In 45BC the Roman lawyer Cicero pointed to the beauty and harmony of the heavenly bodies and stated: 'When we see a mechanism such as a planetary model or a clock do we doubt that it is the creation of a conscious intelligence? So how can we doubt that the world is the work of the divine intelligence.'[20]

The Reformation of the sixteenth century and the scientific revolution of the seventeenth and eighteenth centuries saw the flourishing of this design argument. Eminent scientists such as John Ray and Robert Boyle used it to demonstrate God's creative power, wisdom and providence. William Derham who took part in the subsequent Boyle lectures went even further in claiming that belief in God could actually be proved beyond dispute by the evidence of nature.

From Cicero onwards the design argument had used primarily the anatomy and physiology of living creatures and the usefulness of the earth. For example, Ray's massive work only touches briefly on astronomy—he is far more interested in the fly's eye! When the beauty and order of the heavens had been used it had mainly been as an appeal to their aesthetic quality rather than the science behind them. However, Newton's quantitative scientific account of celestial motions allowed the design argument to be used in the realm of astronomy. Newton himself pointed to the centrality of the Sun, the regular orbits of the planets, the remote distance of the giant planets and the fact that matter is widely distributed and does not fall into the centre of the universe by gravity as marks of design.

An important consequence of this should be noted in passing. Although the Newtonian world-view gave new material for the design argument, it also helped to advance the cause of deism. God became remote, starting the universe off and then leaving it to be dominated by mechanistic laws.

The popularity of the design argument continued in the eighteenth and nineteenth centuries in the Bridgewater Treatises and the work of William Paley. Paley made famous the watch analogy:

In crossing a heath suppose I pitched my foot against a stone, and were asked how the stone comes to be there: I might possibly answer, that, for anything I knew to the contrary, it had lain there for ever; nor would it, perhaps, be very easy to show the absurdity of this answer. But suppose I found a watch upon the ground, and it should be inquired how the watch happened to be in that place. I should hardly think of the answer I had given before— that, for anything I knew, the watch might always have been there. Yet why should not this answer serve for the watch as well as for the stone?[21]

The intricate and delicate organization of a watch is overwhelming evidence that it has been designed. He argued that the argument was not weakened if the person had never seen the watch before, if the watch did not work perfectly or if the watch had unknown features. One could still infer a designer. In the same way, he argued the universe resembles a watch in its organization and therefore there must exist a cosmic designer who has arranged the world this way for a purpose.

It was Darwin's explanation of the apparent 'design' of the biological world through natural selection which heralded the death of the popular design argument in the nineteenth and twentieth centuries. This example of the failure of the design argument became so powerful that scientists and theologians followed its lead, preferring not to have anything to do with talk of design.

It is therefore strange to see a recent re-emergence of this argument in connection with the unanswered questions of cosmology. It may be connected with the fact that astronomical examples are not explained by Darwinian natural selection. As we have seen the singularity problem of the standard hot Big Bang model has encouraged some to pursue the cosmological argument, that is, is God needed as first cause? That the universe is ordered or fine-tuned to an astonishing degree in order that rational beings can evolve has also led some to pursue once again the design argument.

In fact, there are those who will contend that science does not disprove God but exactly the opposite. That is, science can be used to show the way to God. It has been suggested that the growth of the design argument in the eighteenth century had its basis in a decisive shift in the balance of importance accorded to revelation and reason with a swing towards the latter. In recent years, both Paul Davies, formerly Professor of Theoretical Physics at Newcastle, and Sir Fred Hoyle would follow such a swing. Neither have any time for traditional Christian theism but would claim that science is a surer path to God than religion.

Alongside these scientists a number of theologians have followed the same line. Of these the Cambridge theologian, Brian Hebblethwaite states: 'The suggestion that an explicit intention lies behind the whole process finds much support from recent cosmological discoveries.'[22]

This is an extremely strong statement in the light of Big Bang theory and possible theories of everything. The question that confronts the worlds of both science and theology is whether indeed cosmological discoveries strengthen the claims of Christianity, and if they do, in what way? Can the 'designer way to God' so popular before the emergence of Darwinism be resurrected in the arena of the early universe, or should it be left in the grave?

Pointers to God?

There seem to be a number of reasons why physicists have become increasingly open to the 'God question'. We will pick out four of them.

1. Anthropic balances

All of us know that if the Earth was a little closer to the Sun it would be too hot for life, and if it was a little further away it would be too cold. In fact the orbit of the Earth is very finely tuned to the existence of life. It is an example of an anthropic balance, that is if it were different then life on Earth would not exist.

Over the past couple of decades such balances have been discovered at a much deeper level in the laws of physics themselves. We have already described the incredible balance between the Big Bang expansion and the gravitational force, which makes possible a universe of sufficient age and structure for carbon-based life to evolve. There are many others like it.

The very production of carbon itself exhibits such a feature. Carbon is formed by the combination of either three helium nuclei, or by the nuclei of helium and beryllium. But for carbon to be formed, the internal energy levels of the nuclei have to be just right. There has to be what is called resonance. If this resonant energy level were only 0.5% different, no carbon would be formed. In addition, the resonance which would turn all the carbon into oxygen is just 1% too high. If it were 1% lower, once again there would be no carbon. Sir Fred Hoyle who discovered such an arrangement later said, 'Nothing has shaken my atheism as much as this discovery.' There seems to be fine-tuning here in the production of carbon. Paul Davies sees these balances as the most compelling evidence for an element of cosmic design.

Example after example could be given of these anthropic balances from the ratio of various constants of nature to the properties of water which enable the emergence of life.[23] Some have responded to this by the blunt 'so what?'. After all, they say, the universe is one event, why should we be surprised by coincidences? Although it would be very surprising on the basis of probability for me to win a new car in a prize draw, someone has to win. Nevertheless, we are surprised! In terms of the universe, it is not just the fact that there are anthropic balances, but the scale of them that raises the 'why' question.

In order to attempt to address this question, some scientists have invoked an anthropic principle. However, as we have already seen in using it with a theory of many universes, we stray from physics to metaphysics.

Still others keep their faith in some deeper fundamental law that will explain these balances. This should be accepted. For example, inflationary models do explain naturally how the universe is so close to the critical rate of expansion. But to explain how does not take away the question of why the universe should have this property. Why does inflation allow this extraordinary universe to develop? Even a theory of everything does not solve this question.

Finally, such talk of anthropic balances has been attacked on the basis of 'carbon-based life imperialism'! What about the possibility of other forms of life not based on carbon or even on planets? The difficulty however, is that at the moment we only know of carbon-based life. This is not to avoid the point, but simply to recognize that it is all we have to work with. Even if there is other life in the universe, we are still left with the question: why *this* life?

Therefore, anthropic balances should not be dismissed. They are a significant factor in the way the world is, and we need to note that they have led a number of scientists to questions of religion.

Of course such insights cannot be used to prove the existence of God. In 1779, the philosopher David Hume attacked the logic of inferring the Christian God from the nature of the universe.[24] Amongst a large number of logical problems which he raised, one is particularly important for our discussion of anthropic balances.

He argued that even if a divine designer could validly be inferred, we would not be able to postulate a Christian God who is good, wise and powerful. Hume argues that for a given effect you can only infer a cause sufficient to produce that effect. Therefore from a finite creation one can never infer an infinite God. In addition, from the diversity of the world one cannot infer one God. More importantly, even if one is able to reconcile evil with an omnipotent and wholly good God, one cannot infer a wholly good God from a manifestly imperfect world where evil exists. Kant also came to the conclusion that the design argument at most could only lead to a cosmic architect using existing material. Now this is surely correct.

This is illustrated very well by the kind of god both Hoyle and Davies end up with. Neglecting the possibility of historical revelation and religious experience as a possible source of knowledge, they suggest that there is no conflict between a universe evolving according to the laws of physics but nevertheless subject to intelligent control. It is from this basis that Davies suggests a 'natural God' who operates within the laws of nature, directing and controlling the evolution of the cosmos. This natural god produces within the laws of physics a complex and orderly cosmos.

Therefore, the use of the design argument has led to a god who is not transcendent but contained by the universe and its laws. Davies' God is more of a 'demiurge'. This term was used by the Greeks to denote a craftsman 'god' rather than the supreme creator being. A similar conclusion is arrived at by Professor Brian Josephson, the Cambridge solid state physicist. Josephson sees God in the chaotic quantum fluctuations which quantum field theory would claim to exist even in a perfect vacuum. But for Josephson, as for Davies and Hoyle, God resides within the universe. In such an approach the distinction between God and nature becomes terribly blurred, and is reminiscent of the impersonal pantheism of Spinoza.

The 'surer path to God' has led to a god remade to harmonize with the prevailing scientific ethos. Hanbury Brown, the Australian astronomer, has recently stated that this is what needs to be done to religion. The idea of God as a person is dismissed as belonging 'to an earlier simpler stage in the history of thought'.[25] Davies suggests that his god might well be enough to satisfy most believers, but it is clear that this is not the same God of Abraham, Isaac and Jacob.

However the point must be made that even if the design argument cannot lead to the Christian God, this does not mean that it is without value. The insight of anthropic balances within the universe may be a starting point. To use Hume's imagery, if we were able to see only one side of a pair of scales with a mass of ten grams on it and we saw it ascend, then of course from that observation we would not be able to say what the weight on the other side was. However, we could say that there was a force on the other end (whether a mass greater than ten grams or the hand of a person), and this is not a trivial piece of information.

If the design argument as a way to prove the existence of God is no longer valid, then there is still something to be said despite all the criticisms. These anthropic balances may suggest that there is more to the universe than science can explain, and for some this will be a pointer to God.

2. An incomprehensible comprehensibility!

It was Einstein who remarked that the only incomprehensible thing about the universe is that it is comprehensible! We have noted this as a basic assumption of science from quantum theory to general relativity, and indeed that it is central to any theory of everything.

Paul Davies finds this to be a significant pointer to something more and in his recent book states:

> Through science we human beings are able to grasp at least some of the nature's secrets. . . . Why should this be, just why Homo Sapiens should carry the spark of rationality that provides the key to the universe is a deep enigma. We who are children of the universe—animated stardust—can nevertheless reflect on the nature of the same universe, even to the extent of glimpsing the rules on which it runs. . . .

What is Man that we may be party to such privilege? I cannot believe that our existence in this universe is a mere quirk of fate, an accident of fate, an incidental blip in the great cosmic drama. Our involvement is just too intimate. The physical species Homo may count for nothing, but the existence of mind in some organism on some planet in the universe is surely a fact of fundamental significance. . . . This can be no trivial detail, no minor byproduct of mindless purposeless forces. We are truly meant to be here.[26]

Once again, this is not someone proving the existence of God. However, it is for some a springboard into the question of God. Why is the universe intelligible to us? Our grasp of the physical laws goes far beyond what is required for our survival. But it is consistent with a God of order who gives the capacity to the universe of bringing forth life.

3. Awe in the face of it all

It is striking that there is a widespread sense of awe at the universe science discloses. Scientists and artists in response to the beauty, vastness and simplicity of the universe speak of reverence, inspira-tion, and wonder encountered through looking at the stars.

From the sight of the Milky Way stretching across the sky on a clear night, to the photographs of stars and nebulae taken with modern telescopes, there is beauty in the universe. Such beauty does invoke awe, and certainly is consistent with a good Creator God. In fact some philosophers have suggested that a basically beautiful world gives you more reason for belief in a Creator.

If the universe is beautiful it is also vast. In the Old Testament, the psalmist wrote: 'When I consider your heavens, the work of your fingers, the moon and stars which you have set into place, what is man that you are mindful of him, the son of man that you care for him?' (Psalm 8:3–4)

This feeling of the smallness of humanity provokes different reactions. The philosopher and scientist, Danah Zohar, speaks of the feeling of coldness and emptiness, of being alone under the night sky. Yet the astronaut James Irwin spoke of seeing the Earth from Apollo 15 as such a 'warm, beautiful, living object' that 'seeing this has to change a man, has to make a man appreciate the creation of God and the love of God'. This echoes the writer of Psalm 8 who goes on to speak of humanity's significance being found in their relationship with the Creator God. From that perspective, the vastness of the universe is not a source of fear but an invitation to worship.

Some may ask at this point, why is the universe so vast? If God is Creator, then why not just one Sun and one planet? This would be sufficient to support life. Part of the answer is to be found in the previous chapters. We saw that the universe was so balanced that in order to give the billions of years for stars and elements like carbon to be produced, then it needs to be large. However, it is not a full answer, for it simply begs the question of why did carbon have to be formed that way? The only thing that Christianity replies at this point is that the God of the Bible is a God of extravagant generosity. Theology calls this characteristic 'grace'. He creates with an extravagance which reflects his own greatness and glory. Another Old Testament psalm celebrates this by beginning, 'The heavens declare the glory of God' (Psalm 19:1). It again is not a full answer, but it does make sense that the creation should in some way reflect the Creator.

There is also awe in the scientific enterprise itself. If most of science is dull hard work, there are those moments of discovery which scientists, would call, 'Wow, look at that!' moments. The physicist Richard Feynman, though not a Christian, nevertheless spoke of being a scientist as: 'The same thrill, the same awe and mystery, comes again and again when we look at any question deeply enough . . . it is true that few unscientific people have this type of religious experience'.[27]

This kind of response has a long history in scientific thought. Kepler spoke of 'joy' and being 'ravished' at the creation. Einstein, who was hesitant about the idea of a personal God himself, was however struck by the logical simplicity of the universe. The complexity of the physical universe flows from the basic laws and initial conditions which are comparatively simple. That underneath complexity lies simplicity, is a discovery which evokes awe in many scientists. Perhaps it is this that is reflected in the words of Simone Weil, 'Scientific research is simply a form of religious contemplation'.[28]

4. *Hope in a futile universe*

The basic feeling that there is hope and purpose in the world is an important factor. Very few people believe that life is meaningless. Yet from the point of view of cosmology, the outlook is rather bleak. If human life survives such catastrophes as a collision with a comet or a meteor, or the end of the Sun in a few billion years, then there is a further and more serious problem ahead.

Cosmologists see two possible futures for the universe. It could reach a point where the force of gravity acts on the matter of the universe to reverse the expansion force of the Big Bang, collapsing the universe back to a point of infinite density—a Big Crunch! However, there may not be enough matter in the universe to make this happen. If this is the case the universe expands for ever becoming more and more a cold lifeless place full of dead stars. This is called heat death, which Arthur Bloch likened to a giant stew cooling for billions of years so that soon the carrots will become indistinguishable from the onions!

At the moment cosmologists are not sure which will happen as the problem is knowing just how much matter there actually is. This question is made harder by the possibility that there may be vast amounts of matter which we can't see—the so-called 'dark matter' problem.

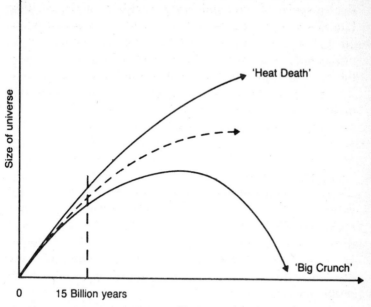

Fig 8.2 The fate of the universe. At our present age of 15 billion years the universe is expanding, but at the moment we are not sure about what will happen in the future. Whether it will expand for ever, or collapse due to the force of gravity into a Big Crunch, is controlled by the amount of matter in the universe. Whatever the fate, it is one of futility.

What is clear however, is that both of these scenarios reveal a future of futility and death. Perhaps unwilling to face the despair of this future, some have attempted to argue that human intelligence will survive whatever happens. The key to this is to see human intelligence reaching such a point in the manipulation of the laws of nature that it transcends the constraints of space and time. From a purely scientific argument that is perhaps the only way you can go.

However, the Christian faith has an important aspect in this context. It does affirm that the creation is good and from God, but it also affirms that God's purposes are greater than just this physical universe. The Bible uses pictures of a new heaven and a new earth to convey both a sense of continuity and a sense of discontinuity with this created order. A universe of both beauty and futility is quite consistent with the Christian perspective.

In many ways, it parallels the Christian belief concerning life after death. In the same way that God raised Jesus to life after his death on the cross, so Christians believe that he will raise others. The resurrection body of Jesus is therefore the foretaste or model of what resurrection life is all about. The evidence of the New Testament makes it clear that the resurrection body of Jesus had both continuity and discontinuity with his life before death. He was physical in that he was recognized and ate with the disciples, but he was more than physical seeming to be able to appear in rooms where the doors were shut. If his resurrection body was physical, it was no mere resuscitation. It was a raising to new life, free of the physical limitations of this world.

In terms of the universe, the old question of whether there is not more to life than death in this way takes on a cosmic meaning. It is in this context that the Christian claim that the fulfilment of the purpose and meaning of the universe is to be seen beyond the physical laws has great attraction. What these images mean precisely in physical terms is unclear, apart from maintaining both continuity and discontinuity with this universe.

Is there anybody else out there?

We have so far reviewed a number of aspects of modern cosmology that either raise religious questions for some astronomers, or fit well with Christian belief. Before we leave these pointers we must examine a question that for many people at first sight totally undermines the Christian faith.

Every astronomer who has ever given a public lecture knows that there is one question that is always asked, 'Do you believe in life elsewhere in the universe?' It is an important question. The whole genre of science fiction from *Close Encounters of the Third Kind* to *Star Wars* reflects a fascination with the question. Corn circles and sightings of unidentified flying objects are seen by some as proof of extra-terrestrial life, and even NASA are prepared to spend millions of dollars on an all-sky survey to search for any evidence of alien civilization.

The astronomer who is asked the question in purely scientific terms needs to be cautious. It might seem an easy argument to say that the universe is such a big place that there must be a planet out there with some sort of life. However, this argument is too simplistic. The development of life on this planet has been dependent on many subtle anthropic balances. If one puts the vastness of the universe as evidence for extra-terrestrial intelligence, then the anthropic balances need to go on the other side. How you then weigh such an argument is far from clear, and various astronomers draw very different conclusions.

To complicate matters even further, there is the additional argument concerning space travel. In the words of the physicist Enrico Fermi, 'if they existed they would be here'. The development of human beings is quite late in the history of the universe and it can be shown that other civilizations have had the time to grow and colonize their immediate surroundings. At present we see no evidence of this. Some will point to UFOs, but the difficulty of this (leaving aside the problem of positive identification) is the following. The journey to the Earth will be long, difficult and expensive. Einstein's theory of special relativity makes clear that no physical object can travel faster than the speed of light. Even travelling close to the speed of light, it would take many years to reach the Earth from another star. It seems a little odd that at the end of such a journey any visitors would only approach people in the dead of night in dark woods! It would be far more reasonable to go straight to the White House for a cup of coffee! To counter this, the convinced UFO believer might say that the aliens only wish to observe rather than interfere with our world. But the obvious reply to this, is to ask why UFOs are seen at all! If they have the technology to travel to Earth surely they have the technology not to be spotted travelling across the sky!

This of course does not rule out that there may be life on the other side of the universe, far enough away that the space travel argument does not apply. The problem here is that if they send a message which takes millions of years to reach us, and our reply takes millions of years as well, it is not going to be a very meaningful conversation.

We may conclude from all of this that there is no clear answer to the question of the existence of extra-terrestrial intelligence. However, why is it of such interest? Perhaps the vastness and loneliness of the universe (especially in a view which ignores the existence of God) means that we search desperately for other forms of life. Perhaps it is a question about our status as human beings. Are we unique, and if so what has this to say about our significance in the universe?

The possibility of extra-terrestrial intelligence, some would argue, demolishes completely the traditional perspective of humanity with a special status before God. However, such a conclusion is not inevitable. The Bible itself is primarily concerned with humanity's relationship with the Creator God, without addressing anywhere the question of extra-terrestrial intelligence. A relationship can have special status without ruling out completely other relationships. The fact that one daughter is unique and valued to a family, does not exclude other children having themselves a unique relationship. If there was extra-terrestrial intelligence elsewhere in the universe, this would not pose a problem to Christian faith. The God of the

Bible is a personal God who wants to be in relationship with his creatures, and so it would not be surprising to find him taking the initiative in forming relationships with any extra-terrestrial intelligence.

What the possibility of extra-terrestrial intelligence does do is to remind us to be cautious about laying too much reliance on anthropic features as a possible proof for God. However, it does not detract from these features as insights into the way the universe is. Even if extra-terrestrial intelligence existed we would still be left with the questions of why our universe is capable of producing life, why it is intelligible to us, what the significance is of our sense of awe, and what ground of hope there is in the face of futility.

From design to designer?

It is interesting to ask why this 'phenomenon' of revival of interest in questions of design has occurred in recent years. The flowering of such arguments for the existence of God has in the past been ascribed to the influence of Greek philosophy, decreasing emphasis upon the Bible or its social function in maintaining the status quo. No doubt the factors leading to the recent revival are complex, but one of the main factors is surely that it is a response to the recent discoveries of fundamental science concerning the way the world is.

The fact that someone like Davies, who is clearly not sympathetic to traditional religion, recognizes that these questions need to be addressed is important. If it were only Christians propounding these arguments then one might explain it simply as a reaction to their recent neglect. However, the insights of intelligibility and anthropic fruitfulness have thrown up questions which science itself is unable to answer. Attempts to answer these questions in terms of 'theories of everything' or anthropic principles, even if able to give an account of initial conditions of the universe, do not remove the metaphysical questions. In this revival we have observed the convergence of fundamental science and metaphysics.

None of these things proves the existence of God. However, in the laws underlying the evolution of the universe we do see things that are certainly consistent with and for many people suggestive of a Creator who wills the universe to bring forth life.

Perhaps William Paley was right when he concluded: 'My opinion of astronomy has always been that it is not the best medium through which to prove the agency of an intelligent Creator; but that, this being proved, it shows, beyond all other sciences, the magnificence of his operations'.[29]

CHAPTER NINE

IN THE BEGINNING, GOD

Will the key to the universe ever be written on a T-shirt? If the answer to life, the universe and everything is '42' then it is quite possible! The secret of a good T-shirt design is to get something that communicates well, is succinct and yet all-embracing. It is interesting that Stephen Hawking does dream of a day when the theory of everything will be available in such a way. This fits well with the popular image of science. It will give us the answer, and this answer will be accepted by all.

In the beginning....

$$a \simeq \int_0^f s + 42n^z - \left(\log^{p-7/w} + 57.39t\right)$$

$$b = \sum x - 3\pi n \left(7e^z + l/h\right)$$

$$c = \frac{dy}{dx}\left[14\sigma - \frac{17}{M!}\right] + \frac{s}{d}(18z)$$

Fig 9.1 The Origin for Beginners!

Christian believers are perceived to be very different. They are presented as either dogmatic obscurantists refusing to take account of the modern world, or they are shaped so much by the modern world that their beliefs become little more than uncertain moral platitudes couched in meaningless religious language. Their T-shirts would read either, 'My faith is believing things you know aren't true' or 'I should have thought my position ... I wouldn't have said what you've said, which I do believe I have said, though not as clearly as you said it ...', the latter being a modern bishop's attempt to say yes!

Of course religion is sometimes like this. In terms of the origin of the universe there are those who will refuse to take the conclusions of modern science with any seriousness, while others will be totally controlled by the prevailing scientific notions.

However, as we have seen such a picture of science and religion is grossly oversimplified. Science involves the interaction of theory and experiment, the role of human judgement and the never-ending search for more refined models. Hawking's theory of the origin of the universe is not yet accepted by the scientific community and if it were written on a T-shirt the shop would stock a number of alternatives!

In the preceding chapters I have argued that science and Christianity when considering the origin of the universe offer complementary accounts, that is true but different accounts of one larger reality. The question inevitably arises as to what the evidence is that the account of Christianity is true in ascribing the existence of the universe to the will of God. Does it simply have to be believed 'by faith' with no evidence at all?

I have suggested that the scientific account of the universe, even with a theory of everything, does give insights which endorse such a providential account. However, these do not give a demonstrative proof. The problem has some similarity with the following. If while driving along a road the car in front stops suddenly, I can of course give a scientific explanation of how the driver's foot applied the brake pedal and this resulted in the car's energy being dissipated by friction in the brake pads. However, it is still difficult to know why she stopped. Was she feeling ill? Had she taken the wrong turning? Did she see something dangerous on the road ahead? The scientific account may help in certain pointers, for example how quick the deceleration was, but nevertheless all those interpretations still fit.

Similarly, simply on the basis of the science of the universe a number of interpretations can be given. Some deny totally the existence of God. For others, the kind of god who results from these considerations varies widely. Some end up with a demiurge, a god unable to act outside the laws of physics and having made matter from pre-existing energy. Others work with a deistic creator. This sort of god starts the world off and then goes away to have nothing more to do with it.

How can we decide between them? This is a basic question which boils down to how can we know about God at all?

A God who speaks

There is a basic problem with God: how can he ever be known? The universe is a vast and complex place, yielding even now only a part of its secrets to the scientist's mind. A theory of everything cannot encompass all of the scientific questions concerning the structure of the universe, never mind the uncertainty of quantum theory and chaos. The trouble for religion is that any God who created such a universe must be greater than the universe. Christian doctrine indeed claims God must be infinite. If that is the case and we don't fully understand the universe, how can we even think about God? How can the small and limited human mind ever understand or know anything about an infinite God? In the fifth century, the theologian Augustine protested against too easy notions of God and wrote of the inability of the human mind to comprehend God. If you can comprehend it, it is not God.

Some conclude from this that to try and understand or talk about God is a waste of time, or argue that such a concept of God needs to be changed. In fact, the Christian position is to say that the argument has some validity. Of course it is true that the Creator God is far above us and cannot be fully encompassed by human minds. The Old Testament strongly denounces the making of images or statues of God for this very reason.

However, says the Christian, what if the infinite God decided to speak about himself in a way that our limited and small minds could understand? This is the crucial possibility that the argument misses and indeed is the possibility that Christians claim to be central to their understanding of God, that is, that God decides to reveal himself to his creatures.

This concept of a God who reveals himself makes sense. Any science lecturer knows the importance of limited and relevant communication to students. The wise lecturer will describe only parts of scientific theories, although accurately and adequately up to the limits of the students' ability. Further, she will use images and analogies to describe the theory so that the students can understand. This has been one of the aims of this book. The picture of the Big Bang that it gives is by no means exhaustive, and assuming that most readers do not have a working knowledge of non-Euclidean geometry or how to write down a wavefunction, it uses images and analogies. The Reformation theologian John Calvin stressed that in the same way God accommodates himself to our weakness. He reveals himself in ways that are appropriate to us.

We can know because God speaks. If you like, the owner of the stopping car can reveal the purpose behind why she stopped. The sudden deceleration can therefore be understood from the context of the purpose. In the same way those things which are suggestive of God from the scientific account can now be integrated with the providential account to give a full picture.

This is the claim of the Bible. It is that because of his love for human beings God has spoken to us about himself and the universe. It is because of revelation that the Bible declares that the universe has the status of creation and. that the character of God's activity is as originator, sustainer, governor and provider.[30]

Can human reason reach the mind of God? Certainly, understanding the physical universe may give us some insight, but Christianity claims that God has taken the initiative and revealed his own mind. This revelation has taken place in history, religious experience and supremely in Jesus Christ. We will return to the possibility of revelation later, but first we need to spell out what God does say. For that Christians turn to the record in the Bible.

The God of the Bible

What does the Bible have to say on the subject of creation? Immediately some will reply that it says that the world was made in seven days. In fact a recent survey of teenagers showed that one third of those who rejected Christianity did so because they thought that Christians believed in a seven day creation some 6,000 years ago.

However, such a view is misleading. There are some Christians who believe in a seven day creation, but there are many others who do not. That is not to say that they do not believe in God as Creator, it is simply to say that they do not believe the Bible gives a timescale. In the Appendix, we discuss the different Christian interpretations of the first chapter of Genesis. Here, let us examine the fundamental assertions in the Bible concerning creation. They are themes that run throughout the Bible, but are highlighted in Genesis chapter one. All Christians, whatever timescale they adopt, agree on these themes.

1. God is the sole creator of the universe

Fundamental to the Christian world-view is the conviction that everything in the universe owes its existence to the sovereign will of God. He is the author of it, and the answer to the question of purpose. The first verse of the book of Genesis states, 'In the beginning God created the heavens and the earth.'

Such a claim has always been attacked, and the writer of Genesis has a couple of subtle digs at those of the time who thought otherwise. Verse 16 says: 'God made two great lights—the greater light to govern the day and the lesser light to govern the night.'

Now why are the Sun and the Moon not called by their respective names? The most probable answer is that in many neighbouring cultures they were the names of gods. Genesis 1 seems to be attacking this false theological idea, by saying that they are not gods but simply lights created by the one true God.

The second subtle dig concerns the reason the verb to create (*bara*) is used in connection with 'great sea monsters' (Gen. 1:21), when it is only used elsewhere in the opening verse and then in the creation of humanity (Gen. 1:27). One can understand the special significance of creating the heavens and the earth, and men and women, but why great sea monsters? Again the answer seems to be theological rather than scientific. In other creation stories, in order to create, the creator has first to subdue sea monsters. Genesis 1 is criticizing this false theological view and asserting that everything was created by God.

The message conveyed by this text is that God is without peer or competitor, he has no rivals in creation. His word is supreme, that is he speaks and it is done.

How does this relate to a theory of everything? It is important to note that the statements of Genesis are primarily theological rather than scientific. They are complementary to scientific statements, and are needed for a full description of the universe. Here is the answer to the 'why' question. The universe's value and purpose are to be found in the creative will of God.

Any theory which helps science fill in any of the gaps of ignorance is to be welcomed. In fact, the Christian distinction between God and his creation means that the universe at the physical level does not have any gaps of scientific knowledge. But there are other questions outside the realm of science which remain unanswered. The motives for a particular character's actions in *EastEnders* can be understood, but there is a deeper question: why did the author write the plot in the first place?

The biblical view is that science is necessary but not sufficient for an understanding of the universe. It challenges the view of 'scientism' that believes that all questions will be answered by science. In this it offers a way for society and the individual to hold together with integrity both science and religion. In recent years there has been a backlash against science in terms of the growth of interest in the occult, astrology and the New Age movement. In these areas science has been seen as devaluing to human life and spirituality, and so has been largely written off. The Bible affirms human spirituality, but also affirms a correct view of science.

If it has a negative word for scientism, then it has a positive word for environmentalism. The universe has value, not because it is divine in itself, but because it is created by God. This gives a moral imperative to care responsibly for the environment.

In our kitchen is a picture of me in a train. Now if you looked at it, you would find it difficult to recognize either me or the train. This is because it was painted for us by our godson at an early stage of his artistic development! It is valued not because it is a great work of art, but because of the one who created it. The universe is a great work, but is to be valued supremely as the creation of the one God.

How does God relate to the universe in creation? Christianity does not see God relating to the world simply as a cause amongst causes, but as the foundation of all that goes on in the universe. He does not relate to the world just at the beginning but at every moment in the universe's history. Thus the biblical view of God as creator includes him continually sustaining the world in being. The biblical imagery is not God reaching out his hand to light the blue touch paper, but holding the whole universe in the palm of his hand.

So what is the place of God in the origin of the universe? He is creator because he is sustainer; without him the physical universe would not exist and not evolve. This view of God is illustrated by the Bible's use of certain Hebrew participles used for God's creative work (eg. Job 9:8, 9; Psalms 104:2f; Isaiah 42:5; 44:24; 45:18). They are participles which indicate continual exercise of an activity. Thus God's creative activity is at every moment in the universe's history.

Donald Mackay uses the helpful analogy of a television image. To return to *EastEnders*, the plot is self-contained and can be understood. However, without the continual flow of electrons being diverted by a changing magnetic field then no 'self-contained' programme could exist.

When the Bible speaks of God as sole creator of the universe it does not view creation as one momentary act, but a moment by moment sustaining of the universe in existence. And this is the case just as much at the first quantum fluctuation (if that is the way it happened) as for the rest of the 15 billion years.

2. God is the source of the order in the universe

What is striking about the account in the first chapter of Genesis is the pattern and order to God's creation.

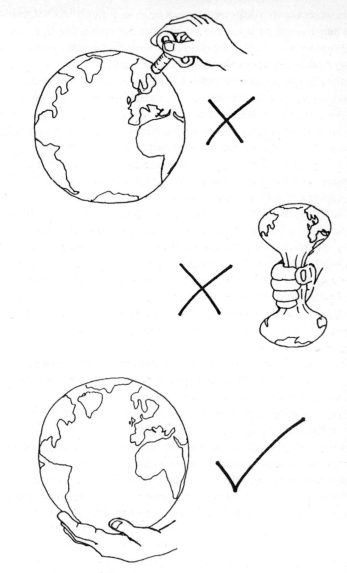

Fig 9.2 *Images of Creation*

The structure of the seven days reflects a logical rather than chronological order. This is laid out in more detail in the Appendix. The first three days deal with shape and the second three with filling up that shape. The structure speaks of the order, harmony and beauty of God's creation. Some scholars have suggested that 'the week' of creation reflects a picture of God as the supreme craftsman.

Furthermore, the number seven is not just present in the days. For example, the number of Hebrew words in verse 1 is seven. Verse 2 has fourteen. Verses 1 to 3 of chapter 2 have thirty-five. The word 'God' occurs thirty-five times in the chapter, the word 'Earth' occurs twenty-one times, and the phrase 'God saw that it was good' occurs seven times. Now one does not need to be a great mathematician to see that something very subtle is going on. The number seven throughout the Bible is associated with completion, fulfilment and perfection. It speaks of order and goodness.

The message is that the universe is ordered and good because of God. Science, of course, proceeds on the basis of order in the universe and our ability to discern it. So Christianity, far from being attacked by or attacking science, fundamentally affirms it. Those who explore the order such as scientists or those who exploit the order such as engineers do so because of God, whether they recognize it or not.

This is a further insight into God's relationship with the universe. The biblical images are not of a deistic god who breaks a bottle against a universe's bow and then goes away after it is launched, but more of God as the hull of the universe, keeping the whole universe afloat and together.

In this way, the Bible refers to what are the results of well known scientific laws, for example the appearance of the stars and the seasons, as the work of God (Job 38:31–33; Isaiah 40:26). God is the basis of the natural order, the basis of the physical laws. In John Polkinghorne's phrase he is the guarantee of the physical equations by which the universe begins and evolves. On such a view the Bible has no place for a 'god of the gaps', that is a god who is simply inserted to explain things that science at present is not able to explain but eventually will.

God is the source and guarantee of all physical laws, including of course a theory of everything. Questions of why the laws are faithful throughout the universe, and are capable of being understood find a natural explanation in God as the source of that order.

However, this raises an important point. Is God's only action in the world to maintain the physical laws? If this is the case, then it is pretty much 'inaction'. The danger of pushing the analogy of the ship's hull too far, is that God becomes totally passive.

In fact the very point of a universe with scientific laws has been used against biblical Christianity. If the Newtonian picture of the world is adopted, then God may provide the mechanism but he has to sit back and watch. The point is focused in the question of miracles. How can things happen which seem to go against our perception of a scientifically ordered universe? It was partly due to this scientific objection that the miracles in the Bible were doubted and explained away either in natural terms (ie. when Jesus was seen walking on the water he was actually walking on an unknown sandbank!) or that they were creations of the early church.

Such arguments are still heard today at a popular level. However, as we have seen science today is not too happy with a Newtonian world-view. The phenomena of chaos and quantum theory, although still maintaining scientific laws, warn us of the difficulty if not impossibility of knowing the outcome. Is it in this uncertainty that God is able to work in unusual and specific ways?

Science does not give a literal description of reality but gives verisimilitude. There is always the possibility that our present laws exclude certain phenomena which will eventually be shown to be part of the universe. Are there deeper laws, on the basis of which miracles would not be seen as breaking scientific laws?

Whether or not these points will provide a meaningful way to talk about miracles remains to be seen. However, they do clearly remind us that we should be more cautious today about too quickly ruling out claims of miracles. A vast number of people rule out the possibility of miracles, simply on the basis of an outdated Newtonian world-view. A better 'scientific' approach would be to weigh seriously the evidence for or against particular miracles. For example, the resurrection of Jesus stands on the very strong historical evidence of the empty tomb, the appearances of the risen Lord, and the total transformation of the disciples from fearful, disillusioned people into roaring lions who gave their lives in turning the world of their day upside down. Of course you cannot prove the resurrection, but integrity demands that we be open to examine the evidence and then be prepared to change our view of the world on the strength of that evidence.

There is one other possibility which may be of help in holding together miracle and law. If God is moment by moment sustainer of the physical laws, then science could be seen as simply describing his normal mode of working. But God must be ultimately free to work in unusual ways.

Imagine parents bringing up their child. If the child is to grow up responsibly then he or she needs to know various agreed norms or rules. If the parents are capricious, that is continually changing their minds, the child will find it difficult to grow in understanding or responsibility. However, it would be a poor childhood if there were not special treats, times when the normal rules were superseded by special acts of love. There will be times when bed-time is normally 9pm but the highlights of the West Ham game are on later and as a special treat (or not, depending on how you view West Ham United!) the child can stay up. The development of the child requires a tension between law and what the Bible would call grace, that is extravagant generosity.

If the order in the universe is a reflection of God's faithfulness in creation, then miracles could be seen as special acts of grace when God supersedes his normal ways of working. This view does not answer all the questions. In particular, one may ask if God does work in this way, why does he not do it more often to relieve suffering and destroy evil? It may be that this more personal analogy for miracles is helpful in emphasizing the tension or even mystery in God maintaining an ordered universe while working in unusual ways for specific purposes.

3. God puts relationship at the heart of the universe

What is the high point of God's creation as recorded in Genesis? It is not the Sun or even a black hole! The high point is humanity. In contrast to the Babylonian creation story, where human beings are created simply as slaves to the gods, Christianity views the apex of the created order as the opportunity of men and women to be in relationship with the Creator God.

In stark contrast with the impersonal views of the world as organism or machine, the biblical metaphor for the created realm is kingdom. Not in terms of a geographical place, but where the rule of the King is experienced. This is a highly personal view of creation.

Some scholars suggest that the Genesis account itself is based on the metaphor of creation as the royal act of a great King. God's creative words are presented in the form and function of royal decrees. The giving of names (eg. Genesis 1:10) is a royal expression of lordship.

In fact the things that distinguish humanity from the rest of creation can be understood from within this metaphor. The phrase 'created in the image of God' has been understood in many ways, but key to it is the sense of being the King's representative. Near-eastern kings would erect statues or images of themselves in parts of their kingdom. Certainly the representative or ambassadorial function is reflected also in the responsibility to have stewardship over the earth:

> Then God said, 'Let us make man in our image, in our likeness, and let them rule over the fish of the sea and the birds of the air, over the livestock, over all the earth, and over all the creatures that move along the ground' (Genesis 1:26).

Human beings are given a unique status in creation as royal stewards, capable of exercising authority.

This picture of creation as the relationship between King and kingdom is then reinforced by the images of the second and third chapters of Genesis of God walking in the Garden of Eden with Adam and Eve, caring and providing even when they rebel.

Christianity therefore maintains that the real meaning of the universe is not to be found in an impersonal cosmic force, or in a mathematical theory of everything but in a personal God who wants to be in relationship with human beings. To be human is to be made for relationship, to love and to be loved, not just with one another but with God himself.

Once again, we are saying that there is more to our experience than just the scientific description of the universe. The object of science is the impersonal. The object of religion is personal. That is not to demean science but to recognize its proper place.

Science and technology, which are involved in our steward-ship of the world are rightly seen as an exploration of the impersonal, but in the context of relationship with the Creator God. They should not be seen as selfish domination and exploitation of creation, but as given to us to grow in relationship. Whether it be by fulfilling our God-given curiosity about the world, or by using our God-given abilities to be partners with him in creation, science therefore has a moral content. Pollution of the environment, selfish exploitation of natural resources, animals and other human beings, or spiralling technology for war and destruction bear testimony to what can happen when science is separated from this dimension of relationship.

This aspect of relationship may help us in our thinking about extra-terrestrial life and miracles. God is fundamentally into relationship and therefore it would not be surprising if he was in relationship with others in the universe. The mystery of miracle also becomes tied up in the mystery of relationship. The expression of love within relationship has many courses of action.

Does all of this mean that God created the universe for relationship? An old poem which is read on many occasions in churches talks of God feeling lonely and therefore deciding that he would make a universe to give himself some companions. However, such a view is not the Christian view. Central to the Christian revelation is that at the heart of God himself is dynamic relationship. God as Trinity, that is Father, Son and Holy Spirit, is the mystery that the early church was forced to from their experience of Jesus and the power of the Holy Spirit. God is in dynamic relationship giving and receiving love. Even before the universe was created, God was experiencing relationship.

On this basis he does not need to create. He creates as an act of extravagance and delight. Why did God create the universe? Perhaps a parallel question is why do couples who have financial security decide to have children? There is no need, in the sense of the children being needed to provide for the parents. But there is delight in creating as an expression of love.

4. God is meant to be worshipped

Worship breathes through the first chapter of Genesis. Indeed, there are indications that it reflects a liturgical form, that is, it was used in worship. It is neither simple prose nor simple Hebrew poetry. However, it is clear that the chapter is skilfully arranged. Each day begins with God's words and ends with the 'evening and morning' refrain, and a number of phrases are repeated a number of times. For these reasons, some scholars have suggested that the literary style of Genesis 1 is more like a hymn than a scientific textbook, a meditation on the work of creation so that we can understand that the creation is related to God.

Whether that is its literary style, its central concern is not to explain the 'how' of creation, but to draw to the reader's attention the wonder of creation. This is not to exalt the creation itself, but as an invitation to worship the Creator.

It is important to note that in all of the places where the Bible talks of creation, it does not examine the question of origins for its own sake. The question of origins is intimately connected to the question of God. In the Old Testament, creation demonstrates the glory of God or the way life should be lived, and in the New Testament it demonstrates the glory of Jesus.

It is this response of worship that gives a natural context for the sense of awe at the universe.

A God with us

In the light of all of this, one question remains. Someone might say, I can see how God provides the answer to why there is a universe, how he can be the source of the underlying order of the universe, of the importance of relationship and the need for worship. But, surely all this depends on accepting the Bible. Is there any evidence that this is true?

Christians claim that God has spoken in many and various ways. One way is indeed in the beauty and order of creation which raise the 'God question'. For others it may be an experience of transcendence, that is the sense of the 'something other' in a real and personal way. For yet others it may be 'the ring of truth' as they study the Bible.

However supremely, says the letter to the Hebrews, 'he has spoken to us by a Son', that is Jesus of Nazareth. This is how God is supremely known. The apostle Paul wrote that Jesus is 'the image of the invisible God' (Colossians 1:15). If I use an overhead projector with an audience they do not directly see the transparency; in fact it is often horizontal to them. However, through the combination of mirrors and lenses, an exact representation of the transparency is projected into the vertical plane which they can see. In a similar way Jesus is the 'projection of God' into the dimensions of our universe in order that we can understand and know him. So in answer to the question of what God is like, Christianity replies: he is like Jesus.

However, Jesus is much more than just an image. The photograph of my wife is not the same thing as having her with me! One of the remarkable things about Christianity, was that the fiercely monotheistic Jews who became the first Christians, spoke of this Jesus not just as fully human, not just giving a picture of what God is like, but spoke of him as God himself.

As the disciple John came to write his account of the life of Jesus, he must have meditated for many years on the true significance of the man he had seen healing, preaching, dying an ugly death on the cross and then being raised to new life. This Jesus whom he still experienced as alive he saw in cosmic terms. When he came to write his gospel he began: 'In the beginning was the Word, and the Word was with God and the Word was God. He was with God in the beginning. Through him all things were made; without him nothing was made that has been made' (John 1:1–3).

This was novel enough. John was combining two strands of ancient thought about the universe. First, the Hebrew idea of God creating by his word (eg. Genesis 1:3) which is God's personal word bringing action. The second was the Greek idea of 'logos', the word in the sense of the divine ordering principle or impersonal rationality behind the universe. However the way he combines them is startling. A mere 11 verses later he writes:

> The Word became flesh and made his dwelling among us. We have seen his glory, the glory of the One and Only, who came from the Father, full of grace and truth. . . . No-one has ever seen God; but God the One and Only . . . he has made him known (John 1:14,18).

The startling claim is that the self-revelation of God is seen supremely in God becoming a human being in Jesus of Nazareth.

John reflecting the belief of the early church was driven to the conclusion that here was the Creator God himself in Jesus. It is amazing that all the major themes of creation were focused in this one man Jesus.

If God is the sole creator of the universe, then that is focused in Jesus. Thus, the letter to the Hebrews speaks of Jesus as the one through whom the world was created and the one who is 'upholding the universe by his word of power' (Heb. 1:3). God the Father and God the Son are seen to be together in creation just as the eyes and hands of a craftsman are together in making an object.

The God who is the source of the order in the universe was seen in Jesus. Paul, in his letter to the Colossian Christians writes that in Christ 'all things hold together' or 'cohere' (Col. 1:17). Yet he is the one able to do miracles and himself be raised from the dead.

His central message was about the Kingdom of God, being set free through a change of mind and trust in him to experience the relationship of love with the King. He is the one who supremely demonstrates that relationship is at the heart of the universe. His life and death were not only a demonstration of what it means to be fully human in terms of living a life of self-giving love, he gave himself for our relationship to be restored. Here is the Creator God himself stepping into the arena of the space-time history of the universe, to show his love and to take upon himself the consequences of our selfish rejection of him.

Finally, he was the One who was worshipped. It is staggering that the worship of the one Creator God should be focused in Jesus.

This then is the supreme integrating point in combining science and religion. The pointers from the impersonal universe raised by science, find their full interpretation in the personal Word of God, Jesus Christ. The author of the universe not only speaks to our world, he becomes part of it. In a man, who was not an astrophysicist and was born 2,000 years ago in an obscure part of the Roman empire lies the key to the purpose and author of the universe.

Through his death and resurrection the Christian good news proclaims that this Jesus can be known today. It is in an encounter with Jesus Christ, both in the Bible and in experience, that one's eyes are opened to the author of the universe, the God of power, faithfulness and extravagant generosity.

CHAPTER TEN

BEYOND A BRIEF HISTORY
OF TIME?

After more than 350 years Galileo Galilei has been pardoned. A special Vatican commission has after 13 years' deliberation decided that the Church was mistaken in condemning Galileo. Of course, the Roman Catholic Church has implicitly acknowledged its error since 1823 when Giuseppe Settele was allowed to publish a book advocating Galileo's position. The present Pope, John Paul II has himself spoken of the astronomer's achievements and suggested that his work had been 'initially imprudently opposed'.

The question now is whether the work of one who was born 300 years after the day of Galileo's death will be opposed or welcomed? It is my hope that it will be welcomed.

The Big Bang has brought us a long way. The question of origins has inevitably led us to the question of God. Science and religion have posed questions for one another along the way. Some have been difficult, some have remained unanswered, but all have been enriching.

As we have traced the scientific account of the universe back to the Big Bang, Stephen Hawking has taken us beyond the equations of evolution to ask the question of initial conditions. His theory of everything based on a quantum theory of gravity has attempted to give an answer to this question.

Such a theory is helpful for Christian theism in that it shows the inadequacy of a God of the gaps approach to the origin of the universe. A god who simply lights the blue touch paper of the Big Bang is a god of deism. The God of the Bible is the creator and sustainer of the universe, guaranteeing the physical laws and acting as the ground of intelligibility and purpose. Hawking may not yet have a consistent theory of quantum gravity but it is likely that one day a scientific explanation of the initial singularity will be given.

A view of the relationship between science and religion which recognizes their complementary nature is well able to value the insights of Hawking or any other theory of everything.

However, to claim that such a theory gives a full explanation of the universe is incorrect and it in no way disproves the existence of God. Even within a theory of everything there may be pointers to God. These pointers fit well with the Christian claim that God revealed himself supremely in the person of Jesus, as the creator of all, the source of order, and the one who is to be worshipped in a personal relationship.

I hope it will not take the church 350 years to recognize the worth of this latter day Galileo, but at the same time to point out that God is still God. He is beyond a brief history of time.

CHAPTER ELEVEN

A LONGER HISTORY OF TIME?

The previous ten chapters of this book were written in 1992. Some three years later it seemed the right time to add to this edition a new chapter to bring the story up to date. After the success of *A Brief History of Time*, it is said that Stephen Hawking refused to do a sequel on the grounds that it would be called *A Longer History of Time!* Yet in many ways, the story continues to get longer. In 1995, Hawking's book has been reprinted 50 times in hardback and is now in paperback. It has been translated into more than 33 languages, and has now sold some eight million copies worldwide. You can listen to Hawking reading the book on CD ROM and even buy a book entitled *Stephen Hawking for Beginners*.[31]

Hawking himself continues to be a cult personality. His recent marriage was front page news, and when he filled the 5000 seats of the Royal Albert Hall for a lecture on black holes, a *Times* editorial proclaimed him a superstar. He is certainly the most famous scientist in the world and his every public pronouncement seems to be hailed with the kind of interest shown only to rock and film stars.

More importantly, as Hawking readily acknowledges, science moves on. If much of his fame has been built on his own popular account of his theory of the origin of the Universe, Hawking would not claim to sit back and say that's the end of the story. Such pronouncements litter the history of science. In 1899, Charles H Duell, a Commissioner of the US Office of Patents, claimed, 'Everything that can be invented has been invented', and Lord Kelvin, President of the Royal Society, proclaimed in 1895 that, 'Heavier than air flying machines are impossible'! These blunders seem trivial beside Thomas Watson, Chairman of the computer manufacturer IBM, who in 1943 stated, 'I think there is a world market for maybe five computers'!

The story of the Universe is never a closed book. Theories continue to develop and change. These changes need to be carefully monitored by those with an interest in the relationship of science and Christian belief. Indeed the popularity of Hawking's book has brought such changes out into the popular arena.

Hawking himself has been active. In 1993 he published *Black Holes and Baby Universes*,[32] and this has been followed by a number of articles and public pronouncements. Alongside this, other scientists have hit the headlines in such diverse subjects as questioning the evidence for the Big Bang, time travel, the existence of other universes, the existence of space aliens and the end of the Universe.

In this chapter we have selected a number of issues which have grabbed headlines in the last three years and have some bearing on the issues discussed in this book. By this, I hope to illustrate that the 'history' which science tells is always being revised due to advances both in observations and theory. In addition, the question we need to ask is whether these new scientific insights change our picture of the world and the 'big question' of whether there is a Creator behind this Universe.

'Big Bang not yet dead but in decline'

This was the startling title of an editorial in the leading scientific journal *Nature* in September 1995. Such a headline raises a whole host of issues. Is the Big Bang, on which Hawking's work is based, wrong? Is this an illustration that science is always changing its mind, so that you cannot believe any scientific theory?

The reason for the editorial was a little less dramatic than these questions suggest. It concerned recent work on the age of the Universe.

In 1994, two pieces of work were reported in the newspapers claiming that the Universe was only half the age that we previously thought. In September, Michael Pierce and colleagues at Indiana University and then in the next month, Wendy Freedman and others, published results in the journal *Nature*. By measuring distances to galaxies in a large cluster called Virgo it was possible to give an estimate of the age of the Universe.

This is because it is believed that in an expanding Universe there is a simple relationship between the size of the Universe and its age. We saw in Chapter Three that Edwin Hubble had discovered a relationship between the distance of a galaxy and the speed with which it was receding from us. It is on the basis of that relationship that the age can be estimated. But to get a good answer, you need to look at the speed and distance of galaxies very far away. The Doppler shift gives the recession speed. What is under dispute is how you calculate the distances, or in particular what is a 'good standard candle'?

One technique is to use supernovae explosions in galaxies. After the initial explosion, the star brightens temporarily and then fades gradually. By theoretically modelling such a process it is possible to deduce the absolute brightness of the supernova. Comparing this with the brightness you measure observationally gives you the distance. Such studies including those in 1995 give an age which agrees with the generally accepted age of around 15 billion years.

However, with a different technique, the groups of Pierce and Freedman obtained an age of only seven to eight billion years. In September 1995, Nial Tanvir and colleagues at Cambridge, Durham and the Space Telescope Science Institute in Baltimore used the same technique to also obtain a 'low' age of 9.5 billion years.

The technique they used was similar to that which Shapely had originally used to determine the size of this Galaxy. By measuring the period of pulsation of cepheid stars, you can easily deduce their absolute brightness, that is the 'standard candle'. Tanvir's group looked at seven cepheids in the galaxy M96 in the Leo cluster of galaxies. By comparing their apparent brightness in the sky with the absolute brightness known from their rate of pulsation, this gave a distance of 38 million light years. Now Leo is too close for a Doppler shift measurement to be made as its speed of recession is too small. But astronomers are reasonably sure that the Coma cluster, where Doppler measurements can be made, is nine times further from us than Leo. Thus with the recession velocity and the distance to Leo (9×38 million light years) the age of the Universe can be determined.

You might be tempted to say, so what? Scientists are disagreeing amongst themselves and the Universe is only some eight billion years old rather than 15 billion. What are a few billions of years between friends!

However, if the Universe is only eight billion years old this is a serious problem because it is generally accepted that certain stars in the Universe are much older than eight billion years. So how can stars in the Universe be older than the Universe itself? This almost sounds like a line from a Miss Marple movie where the great detective is able to overthrow the alibi and see the real murderer!

Yet we need to be clear how the scientific community deals with this sort of discovery. There are some like Sir Fred Hoyle who claim that this is evidence that the Big Bang model is totally wrong. Indeed those Christians who believe in seven day creationism take the same view. However, things are a little more complicated.

Scientists begin to ask whether there are technical reasons why these studies may have underestimated the age of the Universe, or whether the *standard* model of the Big Bang may be wrong. This is not because they are desperately trying to salvage the Big Bang, but because they are conscious of all the positive evidence for it. In such a situation scientists will want to examine a number of factors.

First, the age of stars. This is obtained by measuring their surface temperature and brightness and then plugging these values into models of how stars evolve. This is generally thought to be a good technique. Nevertheless, one can always ask the question of whether our calculation of the age of stars is at fault rather than the age of the Universe.

Second, how reliable are the 'low' calculations for the age of the Universe? The Pierce and Freedman results are built upon the fact that the galaxies they study are thought to be at the core of the Virgo cluster. If they are on the edge of the cluster, then the distance and thus the age could be wrong. The Tanvir group, although working on a different cluster of galaxies, have the same problem. However, they argue that M96 is at the centre of the cluster because of its gravitational effects on the surroundings. More observations are of course needed before final conclusions can be drawn.

Third, these calculations use assumptions about the density of the Universe and a particular solution of Einstein's equations to determine the age. It might be that such a simple model is incorrect. Far from saying that the Big Bang is totally wrong, these results may simply be saying that this particular form of the Big Bang model is not correct. A more complicated form of the Big Bang model may be required.

These are important things to recognize in assessing scientific claims. Headlines can be very misleading if one does not realize the background and complexity of what is going on. It is difficult to assess the reliability or even significance of some scientific claims immediately. Time and the testing of results will often change the picture from first impressions. Perhaps we need to remember the story of how in 1962 the Decca record company assessed the Beatles by saying 'we don't like their sound, and guitar music is on the way out'! Hasty judgements often accompany scientific discoveries. Those particularly wanting to make theological points are often guilty of this.

The Big Bang like any other scientific theory is not without problems. Leaving aside the problem of initial conditions which Hawking has focused upon, there are many unanswered questions. What is the age of the Universe? What is the dark matter? The billions and billions of stars we observe are just the tip of the iceberg. There is very good evidence that over 90% of the Universe is made of 'dark matter', that is matter which we cannot directly observe with present techniques. Sir Martin Rees, the present Astronomer Royal, states that the number one problem in astronomy in the 1990s is to determine what is the dark matter. It is somewhat humbling to realise that for all our discoveries we still do not know what 90% of the Universe is made of! Add to this that we do not yet understand the evolution and distribution of large galactic clusters and intervening voids, and we are reminded of how much work is still needed.

Scientists who present the Big Bang as proved are wrong. It is at best our best model. But despite all the problems the vast majority of scientists accept it as a reasonably good model of what happened. It may need to change as all scientific theories do, but it would need a great weight of evidence for it to change dramatically.

About time

In 1995, Hawking received wide publicity following his statement in the book *The Physics of Star Trek*, that 'time travel is possible'. Does this mean that a future Captain Kirk could really travel back in time to save the whale? Of course, speculation about time travel is not new. From H G Wells' *The Time Machine* in 1895, to the *Back to the Future* trilogy of the 1980s, science fiction writers have examined the consequences. Scientists themselves have speculated about the means.

There is no problem about travelling 'forward in time'. Einstein's theories of relativity showed that time runs slowly if you are travelling very fast or in the region of a strong gravitational field such as that near to a black hole. Therefore, if you boarded a spaceship which accelerated to close to the speed of light and then returned to Earth after what for you was a few weeks, you would notice something very strange. While you would have measured a time of a few weeks, the time on Earth would have been measured in years! You would arrive back to find family and friends already aged or dead. In one sense you would have transported yourself into Earth's future.

Is this just science fiction? In the real world it is very difficult and very expensive to accelerate a spaceship so close to the speed of light that this effect would be noticeable. However, the effect itself is real and has been shown in fast moving particles and even in atomic clocks carried on airliners.

If you can move forward in time, then can you also move backward? This is far more difficult! Nevertheless, some physicists claim that there exists the possibility. The basis of this claim is whether space-time can be distorted in such a way that it bends back onto itself. These loops in the four dimensional structure of space-time could provide a route backward in time.

In the 1970s, the mathematical physicist Frank Tipler suggested that such an effect would occur around a rotating naked singularity, that is a point of infinite density at the centre of a black hole. However, such a situation would have to be carefully engineered, and that is significant. For it is impossible to use such a 'time machine' to go back in time further than the time when the machine was created!

In the 1980s the discussion took a new direction. When writing his science fiction novel, *Contact*, the physicist Carl Sagan asked some colleagues to consider whether it was possible for space travellers to cross the vast distances of the Universe by means of 'wormholes'. Since the 1930s it had been known that the equations of general relativity allowed the possibility of very small 'tunnels' linking one black hole with another black hole somewhere else in the Universe. Sagan's colleagues found that under special circumstances such wormholes could allow the possibility of travel. You could enter a black hole in one part of the Universe and emerge elsewhere.

If this was bizarre, then a further possibility seemed to be allowed. A rotating black hole has a singularity at the centre which is not a point but a ring. If you passed through the ring and adopted a particular orbit you would be travelling back in time.

Would this provide a viable time machine? Leaving aside the difficulties of a traveller being torn apart by the gravitational forces of a black hole and the possibility that a traveller might collide with himself going in, there are other problems! In particular, would such a time machine violate what seems to be a fundamental aspect of the Universe, that is cause and effect? Could a time traveller go back and kill his own grandfather?

Questions of this sort demonstrate just how little we really understand the nature of time. Is there a principle which forbids travel backwards in time in order to maintain cause and effect in the Universe? Or are our notions of cause and effect, already questioned by quantum theory (Chapter Four), too simplistic?

Some of these questions may not be fully answered until

we have a consistent theory of quantum gravity (Chapter Six). Until that time, we might remember one observational fact which suggests that time travel backwards is not possible. That is, why have we not seen any time travellers? If it were possible you would expect our future civilisation to be doing it!

Baby universes born in black holes?

There is a further problem for the intrepid black hole traveller. Travelling through a wormhole, does the traveller enter this Universe or another? Edward Fahri and Alan Guth of MIT suggested that matter collapsing into a singularity at the centre of a black hole could be shunted sideways to create a new universe connected to us by a wormhole. Even on a conservative estimate of the number of black holes, this would mean our Universe was connected to billions of other universes.

This possibility has been of major interest to Hawking in recent years. His work on the evaporation of black holes (Chapter Six) led to the basic question of what happens to the stuff that fell into such black holes. The answer he suggests is that it goes off into baby universes. Now this may not be too good for space travel, for Hawking emphasizes that such baby universes only exist in imaginary time. An astronaut falling into such a black hole would be first torn apart. Not even the particles which made up his body would survive, as they would only re-emerge in the baby universe in imaginary time.

However, the importance of such baby universes has been to add to the discussion of the fine-tuning of the Universe (Chapter Eight). Why are the physical constants of the Universe set at such values that make possible the existence of life, and can a scientific theory ever explain those values? Some physicists suggest that if these baby universes join back to our Universe by wormholes then the values of the physical constants would be unpredictable. They would depend on the number of baby universes which we are unable to specify. Other physicists take a very different view. They suggest that the leakage of information through wormholes actually fixes the constants to only one possible set of values.

Lee Smolin sees a completely different consequence for black holes giving birth to baby universes. He attempts to explain the fine-tuning of the Universe by integrating the theme of natural selection into cosmology. He suggests the following:–

A universe comes into existence which then collapses, bounces and produces a 'new' universe. At each bounce the values of the physical constants are changed slightly. This process is repeated until the constants have changed enough for the new universe to live long enough to produce numerous black holes. At this stage the singularity of each black hole gives birth to a new universe.

In this process, some universes are more successful than others. These are the ones that grow biggest and provide the right conditions for a large number of black holes, and consequently new baby universes. Out of this multitude of universes, one will be fit for life to exist. Our Universe which is capable of supporting life is 'selected'. This is analogous to the way biological natural selection eventually leads to human beings.

Smolin's suggestion has many problems, not least the question of whether the model of evolution can be used outside the biological realm.

However, none of these 'baby universe' insights undercut the argument set out in Chapter Seven. There I suggested that to prove God by design was not possible. There exist other explanations whether they be the anthropic principle or natural selection through baby universes which may give reasons for 'design'. But neither rules God out.

An interesting parallel is the way the Christian church reacted to biological evolution. The popular picture is that the whole of the Christian church opposed Darwin's theory of natural selection. However, the truth is very different. As the historian James Moore pointed out, there was at the time a wide range of responses made by Christians.[33] Some, like Samuel Wilberforce, the Bishop of Oxford, argued against it both on the grounds of science and because he considered that it contradicted the Bible.

However, what is often forgotten is that those who had the strongest allegiance to Christian orthodoxy and the authority of the Bible, such as the evangelicals of the Anglican and Non-conformist churches, offered the least opposition to Darwin. In particular, many of the Princeton School of Theology, which was the source of modern fundamentalism, were clearly sympathetic or at least silent about evolution.[34]

Why was that? Colin Russell points out that it was because they took the Bible so seriously they refused 'to saddle it with arbitrary interpretations that flew in the face of empirical evidence'.[35] Those who felt most threatened by natural selection were not those whose evidence for God came primarily from his own self-revelation in Jesus. It was those whose belief in God rested on the design argument. For natural selection offered an alternative explanation for 'design'.

In a similar way, Smolin's natural selection of universes is not the 'God-destroyer' that some have claimed it to be. It is a reminder that a design argument using the fine-tuning of the Universe cannot be used to prove the existence of a Creator. But orthodox Christianity does not rest on such a claim. This sovereign Creator God who reveals himself in Jesus is surely big enough to be Lord of many, many universes and if he so chooses, to create in this way.

Is your father a space alien?

Professor Edward Harrison of the University of Massachusetts recently put forward an even more extraordinary reason for why the Universe is so finely balanced. He says that there are three possible answers. First, that God designed it, but that answer he argues precludes further rational inquiry. Second, the anthropic principle, but he finds this unsatisfactory. His third answer is that our Universe was created by life of superior intelligence existing in another physical universe.

How does he get to that? First, he picks up on the above suggestions of black holes as the birthplaces of new universes. Second, he argues that due to the rapid evolution of intelligence (which we currently see in humanity) there is every reason to expect that a time will come in the future when we will be able to design and create our own universes. Thus, the fine-tuning of this Universe is to be explained as an engineering project of superior beings. They have created this Universe out of a black hole.

He calls it a 'natural creation theory' and claims that it also explains why the Universe is intelligible to us. It is created by minds similar to our own, who designed it to be that way.

There are so many questions to this that one hardly knows where to start! Harrison is a respected cosmologist, but this theory seems quite ludicrous. Will we really reach the stage of being able to build new universes? More fundamentally, where did these superior beings come from in the first place?

He criticises belief in God for stopping any further rational inquiry, but then falls into the same trap. What can we possibly know about these 'superior' beings in another universe? If he is to be drawn to the conclusion that this Universe is designed, is it not simpler to see the 'superior being' as God? Christians claim that this God, far from being in another universe, has revealed himself in this Universe and forms personal relationships with those who open their lives to him. The evidence for the existence of God is much stronger than that for superior beings in another universe.

To say that one can choose the option of 'God created' and this stops further inquiry is naive in the extreme. It was on the basis of belief of a Creator God that much of the early scientific revolution was based. Far from stopping questions, belief in God can liberate inquiry.

Harrison's work is significant for it is another example of the way that the fine-tuning of the Universe raises deeper questions. However, one wonders just how contrived theories have to be to escape belief in God.

Is Stephen Hawking for real?

Beyond, the scientific community's response to Hawking's theory of quantum gravity (Chapter Six), many philosophers and theologians have examined his position. One has to say that the quality of this examination has been very mixed. This is possibly due to the difficulty of non-scientists understanding the scientific concepts, and the difficulty of using appropriate analogies to describe these concepts.

Some of the debate has centred inevitably on the cosmological argument and whether the Universe has a beginning. Too often the non-scientists make the mistake of saying that Hawking suggests a Universe which lasts for ever. This is not the case. In John Barrow's phrase, Hawking proposes a Universe in which 'once upon a time there was no time'.[36] That is as one goes back in the history of the Universe the notion of time eventually melts away. Or as another cosmologist, G F R Ellis, puts it, the origin of the Universe is separated from the issue of the origin of time.

In all of this, Hawking's use of imaginary time has caused most confusion. The philosopher William Lane Craig criticizes Hawking for being a 'non-realist' because of his use of imaginary time.[37] Craig argues that imaginary time is just a mathematical dodge, and any conclusions drawn from it have no relation to the real Universe. In Craig's view Hawking can say nothing of value about the real origin of the Universe.

However, we need to be careful here. It is wrong to write off Hawking as just an idealist or having just an instrumentalist view of his theory. He is using a mathematical technique in order to describe the real Universe. This is admittedly not always clear from his popular writings. His use of imaginary time allows a description of the Universe which begins as small, finite and expanding in real time. This is a reasonable scientific method, whether or not the theory actually works.

Those who attempt to criticize scientists' view of the origin of the Universe too often do not fully understand the complexity of the scientific method. This can sometimes be due to the scientists themselves trying to popularize their subject. Einstein once said that everything should be made as simple as possible but not any more simple!

If progress is going to be made in the relationship of science and philosophy, then hard work needs to be done on both sides. The ignorance of science shown by theologians and philosophers is often matched by the ignorance of philosophy shown by scientists. The origin of the Universe has in recent years forced the subjects together. This is to be welcomed, but it does mean that simplistic generalizations must be avoided.

'God still has a few tricks up his sleeve'

Is everything determined? If Hawking claims to have a 'theory of everything', does this mean that physics will be able to predict everything in the future? In *Black Holes and Baby Universes*, Hawking seems to take the view that everything is determined but is too complex to be known.

However, in his recent lecture at the Royal Albert Hall, he made clear that predicting the future is impossible. Einstein objected to the uncertainty of quantum theory with the famous quotation 'God does not play dice'. Hawking's response is that God does play dice, and sometimes he throws them where we can't see.

In addition to the uncertainties of quantum theory and chaos (Chapter Four), Hawking's work on black holes once again is significant. When a black hole swallows up an object, the information contained in that object is not accessible. If the black hole then emits Hawking radiation and evaporates, then the information is totally lost. This means that even with a theory of everything we can predict even less than we thought.

Due to the uncertainty principle of quantum theory, space is full of very tiny black holes. As they are very small, the information that is lost in them is very small and so we do not notice their effect. That is why the laws of science appear to be deterministic to a good approximation. However, in extreme circumstances such as the early Universe, there could be a significant loss of information. This means that the Universe is constructed in such a way which makes it intrinsically indeterminate. This is the basis of Hawking's claim that 'God still has a few tricks up his sleeve'!

This in fact gives very little more to the discussion. It reminds us again that the determinate Newtonian world view is a thing of the past. We are unable even with all the laws of physics to predict the future in all its details. That does not have to be the case however with God. Professor Ian Stewart ends his book on chaos, *Does God Play Dice?*, with the intriguing quote, 'If God played dice he would win!'[38]

The big question

Frank Tipler has received a great deal of publicity for his recent book, *The Physics of Immortality: Modern Cosmology, God and the Resurrection of the Dead*.[39] Apart from its rather intriguing title, the interest in the book is Tipler's claim of a scientific theory which accounts for a personal God, with consequences such as free will and the resurrection of the dead included along the way.

Tipler is an outstanding physicist and populariser of science whose interests have often extended to the interface of science and religion. In particular, he has written much on the anthropic principle and we mentioned him earlier in connection with time travel.

His theory of God revolves around his work on what he calls the Omega Point. Even respected theologians such as Pannenberg have taken Tipler's work seriously and he has had extensive coverage on popular science programmes like Channel 4's *Equinox*.

Tipler gazes forward to the end of the Universe. In a Universe which collapses into a Big Crunch he asks the question of how life can continue to exist. He sees life as information processing which eventually will be able to manipulate the entire Universe. This manipulation could produce, Tipler argues, an Omega Point. This is a point outside the space-time of the Universe, which is the destination and haven of life when the Universe disappears. It is this point, 'the completion of all finite existence' which Tipler identifies with an omniscient, omnipotent and omnipresent God. This 'God' must exist as 'life must exist forever'.

In a powerful response,[40] the astrophysicist W R Stoeger and the cosmologist G F R Ellis point out the philosophical flaws of all of this. First, it involves endowing this geometrical construction, the Omega Point (which may or may not come into existence), with personal characteristics. As an illustration, although a piece of rock may remind you of a person, calling it 'Harold' does not turn it into a person! Second, it involves seeing physics as the only discipline to answer all the fundamental questions of the Universe. Third, it involves unwarranted assumptions about the character and necessity of life in the Universe. In addition they point out a number of errors of logic and consistency in Tipler's Omega Point theory.

As a scientific theory it does not stand up. However, what is interesting about it is that it expresses a fundamental human concern about the future. Will everything just be lost, or is there more to the Universe than science can explain?

Throughout this book we have seen how scientists have been drawn to religious questions, whether they be about origins or the end of the world. If scientists like Tipler like to push the science perhaps too far, other scientists are simply struck by a new humility.

Speculations abound on whether in the end Stephen Hawking believes in God. This is perhaps due to the fact that in public at least he will not be drawn. What he does show however is a humility in the face of the 'big question'.

When on *Desert Island Discs* at Christmas 1992, Sue Lawley asked him whether his work dispensed with God, Hawking replied, 'But you still have the question: why does the Universe bother to exist? If you like, you can define God to be the answer to that question'.[41]

I have tried to set out the claims of science and the Christian faith when it comes to the origin of the Universe. In the last three years new scientific theories have appeared, many of which still need time to be assessed. Some may lead to difficult questions for those who believe in God, such as what is God's relation to time? Some may lead to an even greater vision of the greatness of God.

In the end, one is left ultimately with the big question, a question that lies beyond science itself to answer. Christians claim that only God can answer such a question, and in Jesus, he has.

A 'BRIEF HISTORY' OF GENESIS

Few passages in the Bible have raised such controversy as its opening chapters. In terms of the large number of New Testament passages which allude to these chapters, it is clear that for Jesus and the early church they were just as much fully inspired by God as any other part of the Bible (eg. Matt. 19:4–6; John 1:1; 1 Cor. 15:45,47; 2 Cor. 4:6; Eph. 5:31; James 3:9; 2 Peter 3:5–6; Rev. 22:2).

All Christians would agree that Genesis 1–3 gives the basis that the universe has God as its creator, and that everything owes its being, order and life to him. However, after that understandings differ. Does Genesis tell us how God created the universe or is modern science to be believed? These are particularly difficult questions amongst those who want to assert the authority of the Bible strongly. In recent years a number of excellent books have appeared on these issues dealing with all the questions involved.[42] In the following I will only attempt a summary of the different understandings with particular reference to the origin of the universe. In all of this the main concern must be to let the text speak for itself.

Seven day creationism

This understanding is the most difficult to reconcile with modern science but is very attractive to those who want to assert the authority of the Bible. It sees Genesis 1–3 as literal history, that is giving a description of how the universe was created, over a seven day period a few thousand years ago (although strictly of course the actual period is six days).

It is an approach which should not be underestimated either in its force or intellectual credibility. There is a tendency amongst scientists and theologians to ascribe it to a small group of fundamentalists who refuse to use their minds. This is not the case. The influential American Institute for Creation Research and the smaller but growing British Creation Resources Trust have a number of powerful scientists among their members.

The approach denies that Genesis 1–3 contains figurative elements, but is quite simply history. The time of the creation can then be estimated by tracing back the genealogies in Genesis to Adam and Eve, and in this way an age of a few thousand years is derived. Part of its attraction is that identifying the text as history means that little interpretation is needed as to what is history and what is not.

If the approach to the Bible is straightforward the approach to science is not. The question is how can an age of about 10,000 years be reconciled with the cosmological age of 15 billion years? The answer takes two forms, which are not quite consistent with each other. One answer is to argue that the Earth only appears old. This was first argued by P. Gosse in 1857, suggesting that God created Adam with a navel. In modern astronomical terms it means that God created the universe with light already in transit to the Earth from distant galaxies, making them only appear billions of light years away. Thus the findings of modern science are accurate, but they only tell us about appearances. The real age of the universe is only revealed in the Bible. This position is logically consistent, science cannot argue against it. However we shall come to theological difficulties in a moment.

The other answer (often put alongside the first, although

they do say different things about science) is to argue that the majority of modern scientists have got it wrong and in fact science itself points to a universe which is only thousands of years old. Arguments used for such a young universe include a decay in the speed of light, problems with ages derived from globular clusters and problems with the Big Bang. These are supplemented by evidence for a young Earth apparently shown by changes in the magnetic field strength, problems with radioactive dating, the explanation of the fossil record by means of the effects of a global flood and arguments against evolution. Some of these arguments do point to some inadequacies in current scientific theories, but have not convinced the vast majority of the scientific community that our picture of the origin of the universe is mistaken.

This understanding of Genesis 1–3 however has four major problems. First, the chapters which it takes to be literal scientific history have within themselves indications that they should not be interpreted that way. That is they contain clear figurative elements raising the question of whether they were written as scientific history. We will give examples of these a little later.

Second, as Ernest Lucas points out, the position assumes that God creates instantaneously rather than over an extended period of billions of years. However, the biblical literature does not require this. Even in the Genesis chapters God does not create instantaneously. He creates over seven days and Adam is created in two or three stages (Gen. 2:7). The same word 'create' is used also in contexts where a long period of time is assumed, for example in the creation of Israel (Isaiah 43:1,15).

Third, if the argument is used that science only gives an 'apparent' age then there is a theological problem. Is there any biblical warrant for believing that God has purposefully designed the nature of the universe in order to deceive us? If the universe was created a few thousand years ago, why does it appear to be expanding from a point of origin some 15 billion years ago? The growth of modern science stemmed from the Christian world-view that because the universe was created by God, observations of that universe could give us truth in some measure. If the universe is designed to deliberately deceive us then the whole philosophy of the empirical method (that is that science is about observation) and those biblical passages which speak of some limited revelation through nature are called into question (Psalm 19:1; Romans 1:19ff; Acts 14:7, 17:22–31). One may argue that it is our sin which deceives us rather than God's design and so leads us away from acknowledging his truth. This argument has some force, but in the end is very difficult to justify from Scripture. I have yet to see a biblical defence of this position.

Fourth, if the alternative argument is used that modern science has got it all wrong not in minor details but in the major concept, then this denies the work of the vast majority of research scientists, both Christian and non-Christian, whose results have been tried and tested by the scientific community. If one is to do this then one must be very sure that the text requires a literal understanding.

The 'gap' theory

This attempt to reconcile the text of Genesis with the findings of science was introduced by the nineteenth century Scottish preacher Thomas Chalmers. Its 'gap' is between verses 1 and 2 of Genesis 1. It argues that verse 1 refers to the original creation, which could be billions of years old. However, the fall of Satan is responsible for bringing ruin and destruction upon the creation and verse 2 is translated as 'The earth became formless and void'. The rest of chapter 1 is thus a seven day work not of creation but of reconstruction, which did happen thousands of years ago.

This has been attractive to many people although there are not many supporters of it today. Its problems are twofold. Most scholars do not think the translation of verse 2 as 'became' is allowable, and that is why most modern translations have 'The earth was without form and void' (RSV). Secondly, there is little support elsewhere in the Bible that the fall of Satan had such a ruinous effect.

Are the days really ages?

Another attempt at reconciliation was suggested in the nineteenth century by Hugh Miller and still attracts many supporters today. It sees the Hebrew word *yom* (translated as 'day' in modern translations) in figurative terms of an unspecified period of time such as ages or the millions of years in the evolutionary process. It then argues for a general agreement between the order of the creative acts and the fossil evidence.

However, once again there are problems. Although *yom* can be used as a period of time elsewhere in the Bible, it is highly unlikely that the writer of Genesis 1 was using it in that way. This is shown by the days being used as part of a week and with the emphasis of 'evening and morning' (eg. Gen. 1:8). In addition, the agreement between the general order of creative acts and the fossil record is not exact. Trees appear before marine creatures (Gen. 1:11, 20) which is contrary to the fossil record and evening and morning appear before the sun and moon (Gen. 1:5, 14).

Days not of creation but of revelation?

This unusual understanding was put forward by a Jesuit priest Hummelauer and in the middle of this century by P.J. Wiseman. It argues that the seven day week of Genesis 1 is indeed a literal week, but that it is a week not of God creating but of God revealing to Adam how he created. Each day God reveals a new part of the story. This week of revelation would then be the thousands of years ago indicated by the Genesis genealogies, but the creation itself could be over an unspecified time before that. Wiseman points out that this explains some odd features of Genesis 1. Why, for example, did God rest on the seventh day when other parts of the Bible are clear that God never tires or grows weary (Isaiah 45:28)? Wiseman argues that the week is for Adam's benefit and God 'rests' in order for Adam to have time to contemplate what has been revealed.

Unfortunately, this understanding rests on Genesis 1:1 being translated as 'God made known the heavens and the earth' rather than 'made the heavens and the earth'. The majority of scholars however do not accept this as a valid translation of the Hebrew sentence.

The literary approach

This begins with the question as to what kind of literature Genesis 1 actually is. The Bible of course contains many types of literature such as poetry, prose, parables, allegory (eg. Ezekiel 16), fable (Judges 9:8–15), history, correspondence, prayers, dreams and visions. It is important in understanding the Bible to be clear about what form of literature you are dealing with. For example, some forms if taken literally are nonsense. The verse 'the eyes of the Lord range throughout the earth' (2 Chron. 16:9) does not mean that the Lord has optical nerves, but is a picture of God's knowledge and interest in the affairs of the world.

So if we address this question to Genesis 1–3, what kind of literature is it? Lucas points out four elements which are important. First, there are indications that the meaning is essentially theological rather than scientific. For example, the sun and the moon are simply called 'lights' (Gen. 1:16) rather than their respective Hebrew names. Why is this? The most probable answer is that in many neighbouring cultures they were the names of gods. Genesis 1 seems to be attacking this false theological idea, by saying that they are not gods but simply lights created by the one true God. Or why is the verb create (*bara*) used in connection with 'great sea monsters' (Gen. 1:21), when it is only used elsewhere in the opening verse and then in the creation of humanity (Gen. 1:27)? Again the answer seems to be theological rather than scientific. In other creation stories, in order to create, the creator has first to subdue sea monsters. Genesis 1 is criticizing this false theological view and asserting that everything was created by God.

Second, there are non-literal elements in Genesis 1–3. For example, on the seventh day there is no mention of evening and morning which some scholars suggest implies that the seventh day has not yet ended. Indeed this assumption that we are still in the sabbath of creation week is picked up by Jesus himself. When questioned about the sabbath he replies, 'My father is working still' (John 5:17). Or when God creates man does God literally 'breathe' (Gen. 2:7)? In addition, there are many word plays; such as the word used for 'pain' is not the usual one for childbirth but is used because it sounds like 'tree' (Gen. 3:16). It is also interesting that the book of Revelation uses images of 'serpent' and 'tree of life' from Genesis, but uses them symbolically.

Third, it is important to note that the structure of Genesis 1 makes excellent logical sense but not such good chronological sense. Lucas divides up the seven day structure as follows:

The structure of Genesis 1:1–2:3[43]

The earth was		
shapeless	and	empty

Day 1
The separation of light and darkness

Day 4
The creation of the lights to rule the day and the night

Day 2
The separation of the waters to form the sky and the sea

Day 5
The creation of the birds and fish to fill the sky and the sea

Day 3
The separation of the sea from the dry land and creation of plants

Day 6
The creation of the animals and humans to fill the land and eat the plants

Day 7
The heavens and the earth were finished and God rested.

That is, the first three days deal with shape and the second three with filling up that shape. The structure speaks of the order, harmony and beauty of God's creation. This logical structure does seem to indicate the aim of the chapter not to be a strict scientific record.

Fourth, there are also indications that Genesis 1 reflects a liturgical form, that is, it was used in worship. It is interesting that modern versions like the New International Version of the Bible lay out the first chapter in the form of hymn or poetry rather than strict scientific history. It is a meditation on the work of creation so that we can understand that the creation is related to God.

In addition to these points, other scholars have argued that the chapter is really doctrine in narrative mode. The German scholar Gerhard Von Rad argued that it does not follow the poetic mode or linguistic conventions of a hymn, but is fashioned for a specific purpose, which is to communicate doctrine.

Now whether it is poetry, hymn or doctrine in narrative mode may never be settled. The chapter is a subtle interweaving of a whole number of literary genres. The indications above that Genesis 1 is not to be understood as literal scientific history do not mean that it contains nothing which is important either to history or to science. Some scholars and popular commentators have gone to the position of saying that Genesis is nothing but a story invented (or based on other ancient creation stories) in order to give some comfort to an ancient people who lived in an unsure world without the insights of modern science. However, this does not have to follow from recognizing that the primary literary style of Genesis is story or hymn. Real historical events can be described in a symbolic way and Scripture itself has examples of this. Jesus himself describes real events in a symbolic way, in the parable of the wicked tenants (Matt. 21:33–41). Also this way of dealing with events is not alien to our culture. In *King Lear*, Shakespeare takes real characters and events and presents them in story form in order to convey a message. I am not of course suggesting that Genesis 1 can be put alongside *King Lear*. Genesis 1 is from God, but the literary medium through which he inspires the message to be written could be closer to hymn or story than scientific history. This does not negate the fact that there could indeed be historical and scientific insights in it, but it does mean that we need to use care to identify those insights.

Genesis and science

Of all the understandings of Genesis outlined above, the latter one seems to me to be the best understanding of the text itself. That is not to say that the debate is closed; Christians need to continue the discussion.

However, with an understanding of the literary form of Genesis not as scientific history, then the Bible's view and science's view can be easily held together in a complementary view of the origin of the universe. Both are true but differ in the questions that they answer and the form in which they give their answers.

Some people say, but why did God not just write Genesis 1 as a textbook of modern cosmology? Surely, they argue, this would remove the need for all this complicated talk of complementarity and the like. The point is however, that if Genesis 1 was written as a scientific textbook very few of us would have a chance of understanding it! Moreover, our scientific picture is continually being modified. Our scientific picture would be incomprehensible to a scientist of the sixteenth century. How then would God communicate to all peoples, regardless of whether or not they had a PhD in physics or the age in which they lived? The answer must surely be in the form of a hymn or a story which could be understood and appreciated by all.

To others who will be reading this, this whole chapter will appear to be desperate biblical gymnastics—attempting to get the Bible and science to fit together whatever the contortion! I suggest that this may be a little unfair in that we have throughout attempted to be true both to the nature of science and the nature of the Bible. Science does not show us that the Bible is wrong. It does however help us to see when our interpretation of the Bible may be wrong. The different understandings of Genesis over the centuries are a record of Christians attempting to reach a better understanding of the Bible.

SELECT BIBLIOGRAPHY

J.D. Barrow, *The World Within the World*, Clarendon, Oxford (1988)

J.D. Barrow, *Theories of Everything*, Clarendon Press, Oxford (1991)

J.D. Barrow and F.J. Tipler, *The Anthropic Cosmological Principle*, OUP, Oxford (1986)

H. Blocher, *In the Beginning*, IVP, Leicester (1984)

D. Burke (ed.), *Creation and Evolution*, IVP, Leicester (1985)

P. Davies, *God and the New Physics*, Pelican, Harmondsworth (1983)

P. Davies, *The Cosmic Blueprint*, Heineman, London (1987)

S.W. Hawking, *A Brief History of Time*, Bantam, London (1988)

R. Hooykaas, *Religion and the Rise of Modern Science*, Scottish Academic Press, Edinburgh (1972)

J.T. Houghton, *Does God Play Dice?—A look at the story of the Universe*, IVP, Leicester (1988)

D. Kidner, *Genesis*, IVP, Leicester (1967)

E. Lucas, *Genesis Today*, Scripture Union, London (1989)

J.V. Narlikar, *The Primeval Universe*, OUP, Oxford (1988)

A.R. Peacocke, *Creation and the World of Science*, OUP, Oxford (1979)

J.C. Polkinghorne, *The Way the World Is*, Triangle, London (1983)

J.C. Polkinghorne, *One World*, SPCK, London (1986)

J.C. Polkinghorne, *Science and Creation*, SPCK, London (1988)

J.C. Polkinghorne, *Science and Providence*, SPCK, London (1989)

C.A. Russell, *Cross-Currents: Interactions between science and faith*, IVP, Leicester (1985)

NOTES

1. S.W. Hawking, *A Brief History of Time*, Bantam, London (1988).
2. L. Tolstoy, *War and Peace*, OUP, Oxford (1992), p. 373.
3. Pius XII, Discorso di Sua Santita, Address of the Holy Father to the Pontifical Academy of Science, Nov 22 (1951), Tipographia Poliglotta Vaticana, Rome (1953), p. 54.
4. P. Davies, *God and the New Physics*, Pelican, Harmondsworth (1983).
5. F. Hoyle, *The Intelligent Universe*, Richard Joseph, London (1983).
6. Hawking, *op. cit.*, p. x.
7. D. Adams, *The Hitchhiker's Guide to the Galaxy*: The Original Radio Scripts, Pan Books, London (1985), p. 39.
8. The Kelvin temperature scale (K) is equivalent to the Celsius scale but has a different zero point. It begins at absolute zero which is -273 degrees Celsius. Thus the freezing point of water is 273 Kelvin and the boiling point is 373 Kelvin. Of course, at high temperatures the difference is not too important.
9. R.D. Jastrow, Readers' Digest, 117, Oct. 1980, p. 57.
10. Hawking, *op. cit.*, pp. 135–136.
11. J.D. Barrow, *The World Within the World*, Clarendon, Oxford (1988).
12. O. Gingerich, *Nature* (1988), **336**, 288.
13. F.J. Tipler, Times Higher Educational Supplement (1988), **832**, p. 23.
14. R. Stannard, *The Times* (1989), Nov. 13th.
15. Hawking, *op. cit.*, p. 116.
16. Tipler, *op. cit.*, p. 23.
17. Hawking, *op. cit.*, pp. 140–1.
18. Hawking, *op. cit.*, p. 141.
19. S.W. Hawking, Letters to the Editor: Time and the Universe, *American Scientist*, **73**, (1985) p. 12.

20. Cicero, *The Nature of the Gods*, 2, 97, 132–3.
21. W. Paley, *Natural Theology* (1802) in *The Works of William Paley*, ed. R. Lyman, pp. 8–9, London (1825).
22. B.L. Hebblethwaite, *The Ocean of Truth*, CUP, Cambridge (1988), p. 90.
23. See for example, J.D. Barrow and F.J. Tipler, *The Anthropic Cosmological Principle*, OUP, Oxford (1986).
24. D. Hume, *Dialogues Concerning Natural Religion* (1779), ed. N. Kemp Smith, OUP, Oxford (1935).
25. H. Brown, *The Wisdom of Science—Its Relevance to Culture and Religion*, CUP, Cambridge (1986), p. 169.
26. P. Davies, *The Mind of God*, Simon & Schuster, New York (1992), p. 173.
27. R. Feynman, *What Do You Care What Other People Think?* Unwin Hyman, London (1988), p. 243.
28. S. Weil, *The Need for Roots*, Trans. A.F. Willis, Routledge & Kegan Paul, London (1952), p. 250.
29. W. Paley, *op. cit.*, pp. 318–9.
30. For example, Nehemiah 9:6; Psalm 33:6–9; Isaiah 48: 12–13.
31. J.P. McEvoy & O. Zavote, *Stephen Hawking for Beginners*, Icon, New York (1995).
32. S.W. Hawking, *Black Holes and Baby Universes*, Bantam, Ealing (1993).
33. J.R. Moore, *The Post Darwinian Controversies*, CUP, Cambridge (1979).
34. D.N. Livingstone, *Darwin's Forgotten Defenders*, Scottish Academic Press, Edinburgh (1987).
35. C.A. Russell, *Cross Currents*, IVP, Leicester (1985) p. 150.
36. J.D. Barrow, *The Observer*, 7th May 1993.
37. W.L. Craig & Q. Smith, *Theism, Atheism and Big Bang Cosmology*, OUP, Oxford (1995).
38. I. Stewart, *Does God Play Dice?*, Blackwell, Oxford (1989).
39. F.J. Tipler, *The Physics of Immortality: Modern Cosmology, God and the Resurrection of the Dead*, Macmillan, London (1995).
40. W.R. Stoeger & G.F.R. Ellis, *Science and Christian Belief*, 7, No 2 (1995) p. 163.
41. Hawking, *op. cit.*, p. 159.
42. See for example H. Blocher, *In the Beginning*, IVP, Leicester (1984); D. Burke (ed.) *Creation and Evolution*, IVP, Leicester (1985); and E. Lucas, *Genesis Today*, Scripture Union, London (1989).
43. Lucas *op. cit.*, p. 9.

INDEX